Nest Refilled:
A Journey of Grit, Grace, and Renewal

Dr. Omobonike Leigh

Nest Refilled:
A Journey of Grit, Grace, and Renewal

Copyright © 2024 Dr. Omobonike Leigh

All rights reserved.

DEDICATION

This book is lovingly dedicated to my mother, *Mojisola Ogunsina Odegbami*, whose spirit of kindness and tenacity has been my guiding light. Her unwavering strength and profound grace have shown me the essence of motherhood and taught me the true meaning of love. Her lessons, spoken and lived, have been the foundation upon which I've built my life, guiding me through its challenges and joys. To my mother, who has given so much and expected so little in return, I owe a debt of gratitude that words can scarcely express. In all its facets, this narrative is a tribute to her enduring legacy—a testament to the power of kindness, the resilience of the human spirit, and the boundless depths of a mother's love.

CONTENTS

Preface 5
Chapter 1: The Call to Unforeseen Parenthood 7
Chapter 2: The Early Days of Adjustment 14
Chapter 3: Building Bridges 28
Chapter 4: Grit and Grace in Action 40
Chapter 5: Finding a New Rhythm 50
Chapter 6: Lessons in Love and Loss 61
Chapter 7: The Empty Nest Refilled 72
Chapter 8: Navigating Adolescence Anew 83
Chapter 9: Towards Independence and Identity 97
Chapter 10: Reflections on a Journey Unplanned 108
ABOUT THE AUTHOR 118

Nest Refilled:
A Journey of Grit, Grace, and Renewal

Preface

On Thanksgiving Day in 2022, my life took an unexpected and heart-wrenching turn. As I was preparing to host a festive dinner that also marked my 4th wedding anniversary with my husband, Olufunmilola, tragedy struck. Olatunbosun, my brother-in-law with whom I had a tumultuous relationship, committed suicide. His two sons, who had arrived a day early with one of their uncles, suddenly became our responsibility, a shift in our family dynamics that my husband assumed I would accept without question.

Olatunbosun and I had a rocky relationship. It seemed he was bent on defaming my character, and even though he apologized on my 50th birthday, the damage had already been done. The negative image he painted of me lingered, casting a long shadow over our interactions. His death on that Thanksgiving Day overshadowed any plans or celebrations we could have imagined.

It took over a year for Olufunmilola to acknowledge that he had not sought my support or discussed this monumental change in our lives. Simple things, like walking around the house in a T-shirt and underwear, became a luxury of the past. I had to adjust to putting on a bra before leaving my bedroom. Our grocery and electric bills skyrocketed—our electric bill alone was over $900 a month after the boys arrived. My freedom was curtailed; I had to consider who would take care of the boys if I needed to travel. Attending parent-teacher conferences, a task I thought was behind me, became a part of my routine again. I quickly learned I was not smarter than a 5th grader when helping with homework.

"Parenting After the Nest" is a book loosely based on this new normal. Writing has been my therapy, a powerful and accessible remedy for both mind and body. Through expressive writing, I've found a way to navigate the complexities and challenges of suddenly becoming a parent again.

I invite you to read about how grit and grace have worked for us in our loving family. This book is not just a chronicle of my journey but a testament to the resilience and strength that lies within us all. As you turn these pages, I hope our story inspires you to find hope and courage in the most unexpected places. Welcome to our journey.

Nest Refilled:
A Journey of Grit, Grace, and Renewal

Chapter 1: The Call to Unforeseen Parenthood

The news arrived like a tempest, upending the calm of our lives with a ferocity that left us reeling. Mike, my husband's brother, a figure shrouded in complexity and a tumultuous past, had taken his own life on Thanksgiving Day, 2022. A day meant to symbolize gratitude and familial bonds, and our fourth-year anniversary instead became a marker of profound loss and irreversible change.

In the hours that followed the news, our home became a sanctuary of somber reflections and whispered discussions. Andrew , usually a man of stoic disposition, was engulfed in a sea of grief and disbelief. His brother, despite their strained relationship, was a part of him—a shared history that was now forever marred by tragedy.

The immediate concern that surfaced amid our shock was the future of Mike's sons, Jack and John . Boys just on the cusp of adolescence, already burdened with the loss of their mother to breast cancer five years prior. Their world, once again, had been shattered. The question of their guardianship loomed large, a responsibility of immense weight that fell squarely on our shoulders.

The decision to take in Jack and John was not one we arrived at lightly. The nights that followed were filled with lengthy discussions, each of us voicing our fears and reservations. How would we reintegrate into a parental role we had thought behind us? Were we equipped to handle the emotional turmoil that would inevitably come? Could our marriage withstand the strain of such a sudden expansion of our family?

Yet, beneath the layers of doubt, there was an undercurrent of resolve. These boys, thrust into vulnerability by life's cruel twists, were family. To turn away from them in their hour of greatest need was inconceivable. It was a realization that dawned on us not with a sense of obligation, but with a profound sense of compassion and duty. We understood that our lives were about to change in ways we could scarcely imagine, but so were theirs, and they did not have the luxury of choice in this matter.

The process of legally becoming Jack and John's guardians was swift, propelled by the urgency of their situation. The legal formalities, however, paled in comparison to the emotional and psychological preparation we found ourselves grappling with. We were about to welcome two young souls carrying the weight of grief far beyond their years. The challenge was monumental, not just in the practical aspects of daily life, but in bridging the chasm of loss and building a foundation of trust and love.

Our initial attempts at reestablishing a sense of normalcy were met with a mixture of resistance and apathy from Jack and John. The dinner table, once a place of lively conversation, became a silent battleground of uneaten meals and unspoken thoughts. Nights were punctuated by the sounds of their grief, a reminder of the invisible barriers that had erected around them.

Mealtimes became the first battlegrounds in our collective struggle to find a new rhythm. The breakfast table, once a place of hurried conversations and last-minute reminders, now hosted a different kind of gathering. Jack would often sit, staring blankly at his untouched food, lost in thoughts that he couldn't—or wouldn't—share. John, younger and less guarded, fluctuated between bouts of silence and sudden, unexpected outbursts of anger or sorrow. Andrew and I exchanged helpless glances over their heads, our own food growing cold as we searched for the right words, the right approach, that might break through the walls of their grief.

It was during these silent meals that we began to understand the vast, unspoken chasm of loss that lay between us. Despite our best efforts to create a space of warmth and safety, the boys were adrift in a sea of mourning, unable to anchor themselves to the tentative lifelines we offered. We realized then that the process of adjustment would not be measured in days or weeks, but in the small, incremental steps of trust and understanding that we would all have to take together.

In those early days, Andrew and I often found ourselves at a loss. Our attempts to connect and to offer comfort seemed to dissolve before the impenetrable fortress of their sorrow. Yet, it was in these moments of profound helplessness that we found our resolve strengthening. We began to understand that this journey was not about quick fixes or filling the void left by their parents. It was about presence, about showing up for Jack and John in every possible way, even when it felt like we were making no progress at all.

As time went on, our family began to experience the tentative budding of new dynamics. The journey was fraught with challenges, each day a test of our patience, our empathy, and our capacity to love beyond the confines of our expectations. Yet, it was also a journey marked by moments of unexpected joy and the slow, but palpable, building of trust.

Looking back on those initial steps into unforeseen parenthood, I am struck by the resilience of the human spirit—both ours and that of Jack and John. The path was arduous, filled with moments of doubt and despair, but also with instances of grace and profound connection. It was a testament to the power of family, not defined by blood alone, but by the willingness to embrace, to support, and to love unconditionally in the face of life's most daunting challenges.

As the days unfolded into weeks, the raw shock of our new reality began to settle into a rhythm of cautious adjustment. Jack, the elder at thirteen, carried a quiet stoicism that belied his years. His moments of vulnerability were rare, hidden away in the silence of his room or the early hours of the morning when he thought no one was watching. John, on the other hand, displayed his grief more openly, his emotions a tempest that could be both heart-wrenching and overwhelming.

Andrew and I found ourselves navigating uncharted waters, each day presenting a new challenge, a new lesson in patience and understanding. Our approach had to be multifaceted, balancing discipline with compassion, structure with flexibility. It was a delicate dance, one that often left us questioning our decisions, worried we might inadvertently deepen their wounds.

The complexity of our situation was compounded by the need to address the boys' mental and emotional health. Recognizing the depth of their trauma, we sought the help of a child psychologist, a decision that opened a new avenue for healing, not just for Jack and John but for us as well. These sessions, though initially met with resistance, gradually became a safe space for the boys to express their grief, anger, and confusion.

Amidst these challenges, there were moments of breakthrough that offered glimpses of hope, of a possible future where laughter might once again fill our home. A spontaneous game of soccer in the backyard, a movie night complete with popcorn and shared jokes, moments where the boys allowed themselves to be just that—boys, unburdened, if only temporarily, the weight of their loss.

It was during these moments that Andrew and I began to truly understand the concept of resilience. Not just the resilience required of us as caretakers and guardians but the incredible strength displayed by Jack and John as they navigated their grief. Their ability to find moments of joy, to engage with the world around them despite their profound loss, was nothing short of inspiring.

Yet, with every step forward, there were inevitable setbacks. Holidays and anniversaries were particularly difficult, each occasion a stark reminder of the absence of their parents. Andrew and I learned to approach these days with a mixture of planning and flexibility, creating new traditions while honoring the memory of their parents in a way that felt respectful and inclusive.

Education was another area of significant adjustment. The disruption to their lives had taken a toll on their academic performance, a challenge we tackled through a combination of tutoring, counseling, and close communication with their teachers. It was a process that required patience and persistence, with each small achievement celebrated as a victory not just for Jack and John, but for our family as a whole.

As the months passed, the contours of our new life began to take shape. The house, once eerily quiet in the aftermath of our adult children's departure, was now filled with the sounds of life—a constant, sometimes chaotic, testament to the family we were becoming. Dinners were no longer silent affairs but occasions for conversation, for sharing the events of our day, for laughter and, occasionally, tears.

Our journey was far from smooth. There were days when the weight of our responsibilities felt overwhelming, moments when the grief and frustration seemed insurmountable. But there were also moments of profound connection, of joy and pride in the resilience and strength of our makeshift family.

Looking back on those early days, it's clear that the call to unforeseen parenthood was not just a challenge but an opportunity—an opportunity to grow, to love, and to build something beautiful from the ashes of tragedy. It was a journey marked by grit and grace, by the unwavering belief that, together, we could navigate the storms and emerge stronger on the other side.

Jack and John, though forever changed by loss began to show signs of healing, their smiles more frequent, their laughter more genuine. It was a testament to their tenacity, to the capacity of the human spirit to adapt and overcome.

For Andrew and I, the experience reshaped our understanding of family, of love, and of the boundless capacity of the human heart to embrace and nurture. Our journey was far from over, but we had taken the first, crucial steps toward healing, toward building a new life together.

As we stood on the threshold of this new chapter, we did so with a sense of gratitude for the journey thus far and a hopeful gaze toward the future. Our nest, once empty, was now refilled, not just with the presence of Jack and John, but with a renewed sense of purpose, of love, and of the infinite possibilities that lay ahead.

In embracing the call to unforeseen parenthood, we found not just challenges but profound rewards—the joy of witnessing Jack and John 's journey toward healing, the deepening of our own relationship, and the discovery of new depths of strength and compassion within ourselves.

It was a journey we had never anticipated, one that had tested us in ways we could never have imagined. But as we moved forward, hand in hand, we did so with the knowledge that we were not just surviving—we were thriving, together, as a family redefined by adversity but united in love and resilience.

Chapter 2: The Early Days of Adjustment

In the quiet of those early mornings, as the world outside began to stir, our home felt like a vessel adrift at sea, caught between the life we once knew and the uncharted waters we now found ourselves in. Jack and John moved through the days like shadows, their grief a silent companion that followed them from room to room, a reminder of the depth of loss that had precipitated their arrival into our lives.

The task of integrating Jack and John into our daily routines was compounded by the practical realities of school and social life. The boys, uprooted from their familiar environments, faced the daunting task of starting anew amidst their profound grief. For Jack, the transition to middle school was marked by a reticence to engage, his previously outgoing nature buried under layers of sorrow and uncertainty. John, navigating the complexities of elementary school, oscillated between attempts to blend in and moments of painful isolation.

As Andrew and I sought to guide them through these transitions, we too found ourselves adjusting to new roles. We became advocates, cheerleaders, and sometimes silent witnesses to their struggles, learning to discern when to offer support and when to give them the space to navigate their own paths. This dance of closeness and distance, of speaking and listening, became the rhythm of our days, each step forward a testament to the fragile but growing bonds between us.

During these challenges, there were fleeting moments of connection that shone like beacons of hope. A shared laugh at a silly joke, an afternoon spent kicking a soccer ball in the backyard, a quiet evening curled up with a movie—these instances, brief and unremarkable as they might seem, were monumental. They were the threads that began to weave the fabric of our new family, fragile and tenuous, but real nonetheless.

It was in these moments that I saw the beginning of something powerful and profound taking shape. Beneath the layers of grief and adjustment, Beneath the awkwardness and uncertainty, there was a palpable sense of resilience. Jack and John, in their own ways, were beginning to reach out, to engage with the world around them, and to allow us, bit by bit, into the guarded sanctuaries of their hearts.

The early days of adjustment, marked by silence and struggle, were also days of quiet victories and subtle shifts in the landscape of our family. They were days of learning and unlearning, of grieving and healing, and of slowly, painstakingly, building a new life together. As the weeks passed, the silence of our home began to fill with the sounds of tentative steps towards a future none of us could have envisioned—a future where hope, and perhaps even joy, could find a place at our table once again.

Navigating the complex waters of grief and establishing a new routine in our household was akin to charting a course through a storm without a compass. The arrival of Jack and John, each carrying the weight of their loss, transformed our home into a space where sorrow and the mundane intricacies of daily life coexisted uncomfortably. Our attempts to weave the fabric of a new family routine were often punctuated by the profound grief that seemed to permeate every corner of our existence.

Yet, it was in the quiet, unplanned moments that we often found the most meaningful connections. A shared look of amusement over a pet's antics, the comfortable silence shared while preparing a meal, these instances slowly began to fill the void of words left unspoken. They were reminders that, even in the depths of grief, the routines of daily life could offer unexpected opportunities for healing and connection.

As we navigated the dual challenges of grief and routine, I came to understand that our journey was not about returning to a sense of 'normalcy' as we had known it. Rather, it was about creating a new normal, one that accommodated the reality of our loss while also making room for moments of joy and togetherness. It was a slow, often painful process, but it was also one that brought unexpected gifts—moments of connection, understanding, and, ultimately, a deepening of our family bonds.

This delicate dance of grieving while establishing new routines taught us valuable lessons about resilience, patience, and the healing power of simply being present for one another. In the end, navigating grief and routine was not just about managing sorrow or maintaining a schedule; it was about the gradual, sometimes imperceptible, process of building a life together amidst the remnants of loss. It was a journey marked by small victories, a testament to the strength of the human spirit to adapt, heal, and find hope in the rhythms of everyday life.

Navigating the tumultuous waters of a new school environment presented Jack and John with a frontier that was as daunting as it was necessary. The transition was not merely a change in setting but a significant leap into a world that demanded adaptation and resilience in the face of their profound loss. For Jack, stepping into middle school meant confronting the complexities of adolescence amplified by the absence of familiar faces and the shadow of grief that followed him. John, entering elementary school, was thrust into a social labyrinth at a time when stability seemed like a distant memory.

The morning of their first day at the new school, the air was charged with a mix of anticipation and apprehension. Jack, normally reticent since the tragedy, was unusually quiet, his usual nervous energy subdued by the weight of the unknown. John, on the other hand, oscillated between feigned indifference and palpable anxiety, his bravado slipping momentarily to reveal the vulnerability Beneath. As we stood at the threshold, backpacks shouldered and faces turned towards the day ahead, I felt a pang of parental anxiety so acute it was almost physical. Andrew squeezed my hand, a silent acknowledgment of the shared worry that knotted our stomachs.

The drive to school was a study in silence, each of us lost in our thoughts, the boys perhaps pondering their new reality, and Andrew and I grappling with the helplessness that comes from watching your children face a challenge you cannot shield them from. We offered words of encouragement, assurances that veiled our own fears, hoping to ignite a spark of confidence or at least a sense of security as they stepped into this new chapter.

For Jack, the middle school environment was a stark contrast to the nurturing, familiar backdrop of his previous school. The sprawling campus, teeming with students, each absorbed in their own rites of passage, was intimidating. He moved through his day like a ghost, present but detached, his interactions marked by a polite but distant demeanor that kept his peers at arm's length. The academic rigor, a once welcome challenge, now felt like another burden, his concentration fragmented by memories that refused to be boxed away.

John's experience, while different in context, was equally challenging. Elementary school, with its cliques and the unspoken rules of social engagement, was a minefield for a boy whose life had been upended so dramatically. His initial attempts to connect were met with the usual mix of curiosity and indifference that greets any new student, his outgoing nature dampened by the uncertainty of his place in this new world.

In the weeks that followed, Andrew and I became fixtures at school meetings, advocating for Jack and John's needs with teachers and counselors who became our allies in navigating their academic and emotional well-being. We sought to build a bridge between home and school, a support network that acknowledged their grief while encouraging their engagement with the learning and social opportunities that school offered.

The breakthroughs, when they came, were subtle—a project that sparked Jack's interest and drew him out of his shell, a new friend who shared John's love for soccer. These moments, small victories in the grand scheme, were monumental for us. They signaled the beginning of adaptation, of finding a foothold in this new reality.

School, this new frontier, was both a battleground and a sanctuary. It was a place where the boys were tested and where they also found new aspects of themselves. For Andrew and me, it was a lesson in letting go, in trusting others to help guide our sons through the complexities of growth and change. As the boys navigated their academic and social landscapes, they began, slowly, to weave the threads of their new identities, grounded not just in their loss but in their resilience and in the endless potential of new beginnings.

The journey of Jack and John through the terrain of their new life was punctuated by the challenge of communication—a bridge we needed to build with care and patience. In the early days, our attempts at conversation often felt like casting lines across a chasm, hopeful but uncertain if they would reach the other side. The boys, each locked in their own worlds of grief, approached communication like a foreign landscape, treacherous and unfamiliar.

Recognizing the importance of establishing open lines of communication, we sought to create an environment where words could flow more freely. It began with the dinner table, which we endeavored to transform from a silent battleground of unspoken thoughts into a sanctuary of shared experiences. We introduced the concept of "highs and lows," a simple ritual where each of us would share the best and most challenging parts of our day. Initially met with reluctance, this practice slowly peeled away layers of reserve. Jack's highs often involved moments of solitude found in books or music, revealing his need for escape and reflection. John's lows, on the other hand, frequently centered around social interactions at school, offering us glimpses into his struggles with fitting in.

This ritual became our foothold in the daunting climb towards effective communication. It was not without its setbacks—there were evenings when the lows seemed to outweigh the highs, when the table was once again engulfed in silence. Yet, these moments too were part of the journey, teaching us the value of presence over words, of listening as an act of love.

Beyond the confines of our home, we recognized the need for professional support. Counseling sessions were introduced, bringing its own set of challenges and breakthroughs. For Jack, the sessions were a guarded affair initially, his deep-seated pain manifesting as resistance. Yet, over time, they became a space for him to unpack his grief, to explore the tangled emotions that he struggled to voice at home. John's journey through counseling, conversely, was marked by an initial outpouring of emotion, a deluge of pent-up feelings that he had no other way of expressing. These sessions, though distinct in their paths, were crucial in facilitating a deeper level of communication, providing the boys with the tools to articulate their pain, fears, and hopes.

As we navigated the complex landscape of communication, we also leaned into the power of non-verbal cues. A touch, a glance, or a simple act of sitting together in silence began to carry as much weight as any words spoken. We learned to listen not just to what was said, but to what was conveyed in the boys' silences, in their body language, and in the things, they chose to share or withhold. This silent dialogue, though often overlooked, became a vital channel of connection, offering insights into their inner worlds that words could not always capture.

The evolution of our communication was a slow and sometimes painstaking process, but it was also a testament to the resilience of the human spirit—the innate desire to connect, to be understood, and to understand. As we moved forward, the gaps in our conversations began to narrow, replaced by a growing trust and openness. The breakthroughs, when they came, were not dramatic revelations but quiet acknowledgments of shared experiences and mutual support.

In this journey, we discovered that communication is more than just an exchange of words; it is an act of reaching out, of building bridges across the divides of grief and loss. It is a testament to the power of love, patience, and the unwavering belief in the possibility of healing and connection. Through the evolution of our communication, we not only found a way to navigate the challenges of our new family dynamic but also learned the transformative power of listening, understanding, and being heard.

Within the intricate fabric of our freshly woven family existence, the notion of communal spaces carried immense weight. These were the battlegrounds where the quiet struggles of grief unfolded and, over time, where the pillars of trust and empathy slowly took shape. Turning our household into a sanctuary where Jack and John could seek refuge and feel embraced was a path defined by both obstacles and enlightenments.

The transformation began with their rooms, the most personal of spaces, where the boys could retreat to the safety of solitude. Recognizing the importance of these sanctuaries, we involved Jack and John in every step of the process, from choosing paint colors to selecting bedding that reflected their personal tastes. This process, though seemingly mundane, was laden with emotional weight. Each choice was a step towards reclaiming a sense of control over their fractured lives, a declaration of their emerging identities within the walls of our home. John, with his penchant for bright, bold colors, chose a vibrant blue that seemed to mirror his energetic spirit. Jack, more reserved, opted for a calming shade of green, perhaps an unconscious effort to soothe the tumult within.

Yet, the significance of shared spaces extended beyond the confines of their personal rooms. The living room, with its sprawling couch and cluttered bookshelves, became common ground, a neutral zone where the family could converge in pursuit of connection. Movie nights, initially proposed as a distraction from the pervasive silence, slowly evolved into a cherished ritual. These evenings, filled with popcorn and the glow of the television, were punctuated by moments of laughter and relaxed conversation, offering glimpses into the possibility of a new normal.

The kitchen, too, played a pivotal role in our journey towards solace. Cooking, an activity once rushed and functional, transformed into an opportunity for collaboration and creativity. The act of preparing meals together, from the chaos of chopping vegetables to the shared triumph over a successfully baked cake, became metaphors for our larger experience. These culinary adventures, often messy and unpredictable, mirrored our own process of learning to navigate life as a family. They were reminders that from the raw ingredients of our individual experiences, something nourishing and whole could emerge.

Perhaps the most unexpected of shared spaces was the garden. Initially overlooked, this patch of green became a sanctuary where the family could engage in the quiet, therapeutic act of nurturing life. Planting seeds, tending to flowers, and watching them bloom served as a powerful metaphor for our own growth and healing. The garden, with its cycle of growth and renewal, reflected our journey through grief—a tangible reminder that even after the harshest of winters, spring finds a way to assert itself.

In these shared spaces, we found not just solace but the strength to face the complexities of our new reality. They were the settings where the barriers of grief began to erode, replaced by the budding shoots of trust and affection. More than mere physical locations, these spaces symbolized our collective journey from isolation to connection, from mourning to hope.

The evolution of our shared spaces mirrored the evolution of our family. Each room, each piece of furniture, held stories of our struggles and triumphs. These spaces bore witness to our tears, our laughter, and our silent moments of reflection. They became the backdrop against which our lives unfolded, a canvas on which the new chapters of our story were written.

Finding solace in shared spaces was a journey of transformation, both for Jack and John and for us as their guardians. It was a process that taught us the value of presence, of shared experiences, and of the healing power of simply being together. In these spaces, we discovered that the foundation of our new family was not built on the absence of grief, but on the presence of love, understanding, and the shared commitment to forge a path forward, together.

Nest Refilled:
A Journey of Grit, Grace, and Renewal

In the unfolding narrative of our reconfigured family, moments of connection became the milestones that marked our collective journey through the wilderness of grief and adjustment. These instances, often fleeting and unheralded, gradually wove the fragile threads of our separate lives into a tapestry of shared experience. They were the soft whispers of hope amidst the cacophony of change, signaling the slow but inexorable forging of bonds that transcended the mere cohabitation of shared spaces.

One such moment occurred unexpectedly on a lazy Saturday afternoon. The day had started like many others, with each of us orbiting in our separate worlds. Jack was lost in the pages of a novel, his silent presence a fixture in the living room, while John busied himself with a puzzle, its pieces scattered like a metaphor for our attempts at family life. Andrew and I navigated the periphery, engaging in the weekend ritual of chores and errands, each movement underscored by the palpable absence of the familiar chatter and laughter that once defined our weekends.

The shift came subtly, a gentle nudge against the established order of our day. It began with music, an impromptu decision to fill the house with something other than silence. As the notes of a familiar song drifted through the air, a bridge was built between our isolated islands. John's attention shifted from the puzzle to the source of the music, a curious glint in his eyes. Jack, too, looked up from his book, a flicker of interest breaking through his usual reserve. Seizing the opportunity, Andrew suggested a dance-off, a challenge met with initial skepticism but slowly warming to tentative enthusiasm.

What followed was a scene of chaotic beauty. Our living room transformed into a dance floor, with each of us taking turns to showcase moves that ranged from the awkwardly hilarious to the surprisingly graceful. Laughter filled the air, a sound so rare and precious in those early days that it seemed almost sacred. For those brief moments, grief and tension dissolved, replaced by the sheer joy of being together, of sharing in the absurdity and delight of spontaneous dance. It was a connection forged not through words but through the shared language of laughter and movement, a reminder that happiness, though fleeting, was still within our reach.

Another moment unfolded in the quiet aftermath of a stormy evening. The power had gone out, plunging our home into darkness and unsettling silence. Gathered in the living room with candles flickering softly, the familiar landscape of our shared space was transformed into a place of intimate gathering. Stories were exchanged, first hesitantly, then with growing eagerness. Jack shared a memory of his parents, a rare glimpse into the vault of his grief. John, encouraged by his brother's openness, recounted tales of school challenges and triumphs. Andrew and I listened, shared our stories, and in doing so, we wove our experiences into the fabric of their lives. It was a connection made through the sharing of stories, a realization that each memory, each shared piece of our past, was a step toward understanding and acceptance.

These moments of connection, though simple, were profound in their impact. They served as beacons, guiding us through the complexities of forming a new family identity. They reminded us that connection does not always require grand gestures or perfectly articulated words. Sometimes, it's found in the shared laughter over clumsy dance moves, in the collective storytelling by candlelight, or in the silent agreement to just be in each other's presence.

As we traversed the ever-changing terrain of our family journey, these instances emerged as the touchstones against which we gauged our advancement. They served as affirmations of the indomitable spirit of the human heart, showcasing its ability to discover happiness and camaraderie amidst sorrow. Through these pivotal junctures, we gleaned that fostering a family transcends mere adjustment to change; it entails forging arenas for bonding, for the collective moments that unite us, and for the love that flourishes, subtly yet steadfastly, within the fertile soil of shared empathy and kindness.

As we navigated the intricate dance of blending our lives with Jack and John's, the concept of resilience emerged not just as a theme, but as the very bedrock of our journey. Reflections on resilience, in this context, transcend the mere ability to withstand adversity; they encompass the profound transformations that occur within the soul when confronted with the unimaginable.

Resilience, we discovered, was not a static trait possessed by the few but a dynamic process that unfolded in the face of challenges. It was in the quiet moments of despair, when the path forward seemed obscured by shadows, that the true nature of resilience revealed itself. It was a force that propelled us not to evade the darkness but to navigate through it, guided by the faint light of hope that flickered in the distance.

Collectively, we were tested in myriad ways, from the logistical hurdles of integrating Jack and John into our lives to the emotional commonality of grieving a shared loss while striving to build new connections. Each day presented a tapestry of trials, from the mundane to the monumental, weaving a narrative of strength forged in the crucible of shared adversity.

In reflecting on the resilience of Jack and John, I am continually awestruck by their capacity for growth and adaptation. Thrust into a world irrevocably altered, they faced the dual challenges of mourning their lost parents and adapting to a new family structure. John and Jack became a force that manifested in their willingness to embrace change, to engage with their grief rather than recoil from it, and to slowly open their hearts to the possibility of new bonds of affection and trust.

For Andrew and me, resilience took on a different hue. It was found in the patience to understand the boys' silent language of grief, in the strength to provide stability during our own emotional storms, and in the courage to reimagine our family identity. It was also in recognizing that we, too, needed moments of vulnerability, that seeking support and allowing ourselves to grieve was not a sign of weakness but a testament to the complexity of human strength.

Resilience was woven into the very fabric of our daily lives, evident in the routines we established, the traditions we began to form, and the spaces we created for healing and laughter. It was present in our efforts to communicate, to connect, and to care for one another in a world that had shifted Beneath our feet.

Perhaps most profoundly, our reflections have led to an understanding that this quality is intrinsically linked to love. It is loving that fuels resilience, that transforms it from a mere survival mechanism into a vibrant force for growth and renewal. Love for Jack and John motivated us to push beyond our limits, to confront our fears and uncertainties, and to build a family grounded in the principles of acceptance, support, and mutual respect.

As I look back on the path we have traveled, I see that it is not just about the ability to bounce back; it is about moving forward, transformed, and strengthened by the trials we have faced. It is about the bonds of love and understanding that have deepened through shared adversity, becoming the enduring legacy of our journey together.

Our reflections are, ultimately, reflections on the human capacity for hope and renewal. They remind us that even in the face of the greatest losses, the spirit can thrive, nurtured by the bonds of family and the unyielding belief in the possibility of a brighter tomorrow. In embracing resilience, we embrace the full spectrum of our humanity, recognizing that it is through the challenges we face that we discover our true strength and the depth of our capacity to love.

The challenges of those initial months taught us that family is not just a matter of blood or obligation, but a choice made every day to stand together, to support one another, and to build a future, however uncertain it may seem. Our story, marked by the grief of what was lost and the hope of what was being built, was just beginning.

Chapter 3: Building Bridges

In the nascent stages of our journey as a reconfigured family, the gulf between us and the boys seemed vast, an expanse filled with grief, misunderstandings, and the silent yearnings of hearts in turmoil.

Recognizing the need for bridges to span these divides, we turned towards creating shared rituals, hoping to find our common language not in words, but in the actions that speak of care and inclusion. Saturday mornings became our canvas, a time reserved for family outings—be it a walk in the park, a visit to a museum, or simply a drive with no destination in mind. These excursions, though initially marked by reluctance, gradually unfurled into opportunities for casual conversations, shared laughter, and the quiet companionship that speaks volumes.

Parallel to these efforts, we introduced the practice of family meetings—not as sessions for airing grievances, but as platforms for dreaming together. Here, seated in the circle of our making, we shared our hopes for the future, however modest or grand. Jack, with a hesitance that slowly waned, spoke of his wish to learn the guitar, a revelation that opened a door to his inner world, rich with unspoken dreams. John, ever the more outward in his emotions, expressed a simpler, yet no less poignant desire for a family movie night where he could pick the films.

These shared dreams and activities became our bridge across the emotional chasm that had defined our early days. Yet, it was in the realm of counseling that we found our keel. Guided by a compassionate professional, our sessions became a crucible for transformation—a space where vulnerabilities could be voiced without fear, where misunderstandings were untangled with patience, and where the boys could see their grief mirrored and validated not just by Andrew and me, but by an empathetic outsider.

The journey of building bridges is fraught with setbacks, moments when the old silences threaten to resurface, when the gap seems to widen once again under the strain of unmet expectations or the simple, painful reminders of the past. Yet, it is in these moments that our commitment to this journey is tested and reaffirmed.

Through these strategies—our shared rituals, our collective dreaming, and our guided explorations of grief and hope—we began to weave a fragile web of trust and understanding. A web that, with time, patience, and the resilience born of shared love and struggle, promised to hold us together as a family, transformed but unbroken.

In the evolving narrative of our family, the conscious effort to build trust through shared rituals and activities became a cornerstone of our journey towards healing and unity. Recognizing the power of these shared experiences, we set out to create a tapestry of routines and traditions that would not only bridge the gaps between us but also foster a sense of belonging and mutual understanding.

One of the first rituals we introduced was the family meal. Beyond the act of eating together, we transformed our dinners into a time for sharing the highs and lows of our day. This practice, initially met with skepticism, gradually became a cherished part of our routine. It provided a structured opportunity for each of us to voice our successes and challenges, lending insight into our individual worlds. These moments around the table became sacred, a space where vulnerabilities were shared with the understanding that they would be met with empathy and support.

Weekend adventures became another pillar of our strategy to build trust. Whether it was walking in the park, exploring local museums, or spontaneous road trips, these activities were designed not just for entertainment but as vehicles for communication and bonding. These excursions offered natural opportunities for casual conversations, allowing us to step away from the formalities of home and engage with each other in new and often enlightening contexts. The shared experiences and memories created during these times served as a reminder of our collective journey and the new memories we were building together.

In addition to these internal family efforts, we recognized the importance of external support systems in facilitating deeper dialogue and understanding. Counseling played a pivotal role in this aspect, providing a neutral space where feelings and thoughts could be expressed without judgment. For Jack and John, individual sessions offered a safe environment to explore their grief and fears, while family therapy sessions helped us understand how to communicate more effectively with each other. These sessions were instrumental in breaking down walls, allowing us to address underlying tensions and misunderstandings in a constructive manner.

Counseling also offered us valuable tools and strategies to enhance our communication outside of therapy. We learned the importance of active listening—of being fully present with each other, of acknowledging feelings without immediately offering solutions, and of validating each other's experiences. These skills, honed in the counseling room, became vital practices in our daily interactions, transforming the way we related to each other on a fundamental level.

Perhaps most significantly, these strategies for building trust underscored the importance of consistency and patience. Trust was not built in a day; it was the result of countless shared moments, of persistently showing up for each other, and of the willingness to be vulnerable and open, even when it felt most challenging. It was about creating a family culture where each member felt seen, heard, and valued.

As we reflected on our progress, it became clear that these strategies were not just about overcoming the initial barriers to trust; they were about laying the foundation for a deeper, more enduring connection. Through the deliberate creation of shared rituals, the embracing of adventure and new experiences, and the support of counseling, we were not just building trust—we were weaving the very fabric of our family, imbued with the strength of understanding, the resilience of shared challenges, and the warmth of unconditional love.

Amidst the gradual and often challenging process of building trust and understanding within our newly formed family, there were pivotal moments of breakthrough that illuminated our path forward. These instances, though sometimes fleeting, had a profound impact on the dynamics of our relationships, serving as beacons of progress and deepening the bonds that tethered us together.

One such moment unfolded unexpectedly one weekend, centered around a shared family project. The task was simple: to repaint the living room. Yet, as we donned our paint-splattered clothes and armed ourselves with brushes and rollers, the atmosphere was charged with a sense of collective purpose that transcended the mundane nature of the task at hand. Laughter and light-hearted banter filled the air, punctuated by the occasional splatter of paint that missed its mark. It was in this chaos of creativity that Jack and John began to emerge from their shells, engaging with us not as guardians and wards but as co-conspirators in a grand, messy adventure.

The project, initially intended to brighten the walls of our home, did far more than transform a physical space. It acted as a metaphor for our family's journey, each stroke of the brush a testament to our ability to work together, to create something new and beautiful from the blank canvas of our collective experiences. The pride in our shared accomplishment was palpable, not just in the finished product, but in the newfound ease between us. This breakthrough, born from a simple act of collaboration, marked a significant shift in our relationship dynamics, signaling a move towards greater openness and mutual engagement.

Another moment of breakthrough came through a particularly open conversation that took place one evening, as twilight cast long shadows across our living room. The discussion began tentatively, with Jack sharing his apprehensions about an upcoming school event. As he spoke, his voice laced with uncertainty, it became a gateway for a deeper exchange. John, taking a cue from his brother, voiced his own fears about fitting in, his words a mixture of vulnerability and hope.

This conversation, unlike any we had had before, marked a turning point in our family's emotional landscape. For the first time, the boys expressed their fears and hopes without the shadow of reservation, allowing us to offer support not just as caregivers, but as trusted confidants. The impact of this open dialogue on our overall family atmosphere was transformative. A new level of trust infused our interactions, paving the way for more honest and meaningful exchanges. The air in our home felt lighter, charged with a sense of understanding and acceptance that had previously eluded us.

These moments of breakthrough, whether through shared activities or open conversations, served as milestones in our journey towards becoming a unified family. They reminded us that trust and understanding are not just built through the passage of time, but through the quality of our interactions and the willingness to embrace vulnerability. Each breakthrough, each shared success or heartfelt conversation, wove a stronger thread into the fabric of our relationships, enriching the tapestry of our family life with layers of depth, warmth, and resilience.

The significance of these breakthrough moments extended beyond the immediate joy or relief they brought. They were indicative of the underlying strength and potential within our family, a testament to the capacity for growth, connection, and renewal even in the face of profound challenges. Through these experiences, we've discovered that breakthroughs are not merely moments to celebrate. They are pivotal moments that guide us toward deeper and more enduring relationships, shaping our home into a sanctuary of mutual respect, understanding, and, ultimately, love.

As our family navigated the intricate process of integration and healing, the journey of deepening our understanding of one another's pasts, fears, and hopes became a pivotal aspect of our evolution. This exploration was not a linear path but a layered discovery, where each revelation peeled back the complex veneers of grief, resilience, and longing that each of us carried.

Jack and John, each bearing the weight of their losses, gradually began to unveil the tapestry of their past experiences, their narratives rich with memories of their parents, snippets of joy overshadowed by the pall of sorrow. In sharing these stories, they offered us a window into their souls, a glimpse of the vulnerability and strength that resided within. For Andrew and me, this was not just an opportunity to know them better but a sacred trust, an invitation to bear witness to their pain and their love.

Our discussions often took place in the quiet sanctity of the evening when the world outside seemed to hold its breath, allowing space for the words that needed to be spoken. It was during these times that Jack spoke of his mother's laughter, a sound he feared he was forgetting. John shared his longing for the mundane moments with his father, the everyday adventures that seemed inconsequential until they were no more. These confessions, heavy with longing, were met with our own stories, our memories of loved ones lost, and our admissions of fear and hope.

This mutual exchange of vulnerabilities acted as a catalyst for a deeper sense of empathy and connection within our family. It underscored the universal nature of grief and the unique ways in which each of us navigates our pain. Understanding the depths of Jack and John's fears and hopes allowed us to tailor our support more effectively, to be mindful of the triggers that might cause pain, and to celebrate the memories and aspirations that brought them comfort.

However, this journey of deepening understanding was not without its challenges. There were moments when the revelations brought to the surface emotions that were difficult to process, leading to tension and misunderstandings. An offhand comment might reopen old wounds, or a well-intentioned question could be perceived as an intrusion. These instances tested the fragile bonds we were building, forcing us to confront the complexities of our evolving relationships.

The resolution to these challenges lay in the very foundation of empathy and communication we were striving to build. We learned to navigate these turbulent waters through open dialogue, where misunderstandings were addressed with honesty and compassion. We adopted a practice of reflective listening, ensuring that each person felt heard and validated, even in disagreement. This approach not only resolved conflicts but also reinforced our commitment to understanding and supporting each other, further deepening our familial bonds.

The revelations of our pasts, fears, and hopes, and the challenges they brought, ultimately contributed to a richer, more empathetic family dynamic. They highlighted the importance of vulnerability as a bridge to connection, reminding us that true understanding requires not just the sharing of stories but the willingness to listen, to empathize, and to grow together. Through this journey, we discovered that empathy is the cornerstone of connection, a powerful force that transforms individual experiences of pain and hope into a collective tapestry of resilience and love.

Navigating the intricate landscape of our newly formed family, we encountered our fair share of conflicts and misunderstandings, each serving as a critical juncture in our journey towards cohesion and understanding. These challenges, while daunting, presented invaluable opportunities for growth and learning, enabling us to forge deeper connections through the resolution process.

One particular incident that stands out involved Jack, who had grown increasingly withdrawn, his participation in family activities diminishing. This change culminated in a heated argument one evening when Jack refused to join a planned family outing, expressing his frustration in a manner that left us all startled and hurt. The conflict laid bare the underlying tensions that had been simmering Beneath the surface, revealing gaps in our communication, and understanding.

In the aftermath, recognizing the need for resolution, we opted for a strategy centered on open dialogue and empathy. We initiated a family meeting, not with the intention of admonishing, but with the aim of understanding the root of Jack's withdrawal and frustration. This meeting was a turning point, a facilitated space where Jack felt heard and supported in sharing his feelings of being overwhelmed by the expectations placed upon him, a revelation that prompted a broader discussion about pressure, grief, and the pace of our integration efforts.

The resolution to this conflict was multifaceted. Firstly, we agreed on the importance of individual space and the recognition that participation in family activities should be encouraged but not mandated. This acknowledgment was crucial in respecting Jack's need for autonomy while also reinforcing the value we placed on family time. Secondly, we implemented regular check-ins, a practice that allowed each family member to voice their feelings and concerns in a structured, supportive environment, thereby preemptively addressing potential sources of conflict.

This incident, and others like it, underscored the importance of flexibility and patience in our approach to family dynamics. We learned that resolutions are not about finding quick fixes but about engaging in the slow, sometimes challenging process of negotiation and compromise. It highlighted the need for clear communication, where expectations and boundaries are articulated and respected, and where each person's voice is given equal weight in the decision-making process.

Moreover, the process of addressing and overcoming these challenges taught us the value of empathy as a tool for conflict resolution. By striving to understand the emotional underpinnings of each other's reactions and behaviors, we were able to respond with compassion rather than frustration, paving the way for more constructive outcomes.

The journey through these challenges and resolutions brought into sharp relief the complexity of building a harmonious family life from disparate pieces. Yet, it also illuminated the path forward, one marked by mutual respect, open communication, and the unyielding commitment to support each other through the ebbs and flows of emotional growth.

In reflecting on these experiences, we recognized that conflicts, while inherently uncomfortable, are not insurmountable barriers but rather stepping stones towards deeper understanding and connection. They are reminders of the ongoing work required to maintain and nurture family relationships, teaching us that the essence of family lies not in the absence of conflict, but in the collective effort to resolve, to understand, and ultimately, to grow together.

As the seasons shifted, marking another turn in the journey of our redefined family, reflections on the progress we'd made together invited a mix of gratitude, introspection, and forward-looking determination. This journey, embarked upon under the shadow of grief and the challenge of unforeseen responsibility, had evolved into a testament to the resilience of the human spirit and the boundless capacity for growth and understanding.

In retrospect, the landscape of our family life had been transformed in ways both subtle and profound. The early days, characterized by a tentative dance around each other's emotions and the palpable presence of loss, now seemed like a distant memory. In its place stood a family unit not defined by the absence left in the wake of tragedy but by the rich tapestry of connections we had woven together through countless shared moments, challenges confronted, and obstacles overcome.

Acknowledging the ongoing nature of our journey was crucial. Trust and understanding, we had learned, were not destinations to be reached but paths to be continuously navigated. Each day presented new opportunities to deepen our bonds, to learn more about each other, and to strengthen the foundation upon which our family stood. This acknowledgment did not diminish the milestones we had achieved; rather, it highlighted the beauty of our continuous evolution and the ever-present potential for growth.

Celebrating these milestones became an integral part of our journey. From the simple joys of shared laughter over a meal to the significant achievements of Jack and John in school and personal development, each milestone was a beacon of our collective progress. These celebrations, whether through small family rituals or quiet moments of acknowledgment, served not only as reminders of how far we had come but also as fuel for the journey still ahead. They reminded us that progress, in the context of rebuilding and healing, was not linear but a mosaic of victories, setbacks, and steadfast perseverance.

Setting intentions for continued growth was both a commitment and a declaration of hope. We recognized that the path forward would hold its share of challenges, that the complexities of human emotions and relationships would continue to test the strength and resilience of our bonds. Yet, armed with the lessons of the past and the insights gained from each hurdle surmounted, we looked to the future with a sense of purpose. Our intentions were rooted in the values we had cultivated as a family—open communication, mutual respect, and unconditional support. We committed to maintaining the rituals that had brought us closer, to seeking new experiences that would broaden our horizons, and to supporting each other's individual journeys of growth and discovery.

Reflecting on our progress was not just an exercise in gratitude; it was a reaffirmation of our capacity to adapt, to love, and to build something beautiful from the fragments of loss and change. It underscored the dynamic nature of family—not as a static entity defined by blood or circumstance but as a living, breathing ecosystem that thrives on the nourishment of shared experiences, empathy, and the collective will to move forward, together.

As we stood on the threshold of the next chapter in our family's story, our reflections on progress were tinged with a sense of quiet optimism. The road ahead would undoubtedly hold its share of challenges, but we faced them as a united front, strengthened by the trials we had overcome and buoyed by the love that had grown, against all odds, in the heart of our shared journey.

Chapter 4: Grit and Grace in Action

In the evolving story of our family, the fabric of our collective journey has been woven with the intricate threads of grit and grace, a pattern that reflects our resilience and capacity for growth in the face of adversity.

Navigating the emotional landscapes of Jack and John, with their peaks of anger and valleys of sorrow, demanded of us a resilience that extended beyond mere endurance. It called for a grace that was both a gift and a challenge—to remain steadfast in the storm of their grief, to offer unwavering support without the expectation of immediate healing. It was in these moments, when words fell short and the weight of their pain felt insurmountable, that we learned the true meaning of grace: the quiet strength to hold space for their emotions, to listen with hearts wide open, understanding that healing is not a destination but a journey we embark on together.

Equally, confronting our feelings towards Mike required a journey through the complexities of grief and forgiveness. It was a process that tested the limits of our compassion, pushing us to find grace in our hearts for a man whose actions had left deep scars. This path towards understanding and forgiveness was fraught with challenges, yet it underscored the transformative power of grace in healing old wounds and paving the way for new beginnings.

It is a vivid reminder that, even in our darkest moments, there is an inherent power in vulnerability, in extending and receiving grace, that can lead to profound growth and understanding. Through these trials, we have not only faced our challenges but have been irrevocably changed by them, emerging stronger, more connected, and deeply grateful for the journey.

Navigating the emotional tumult of Jack and John's grief was akin to walking through a storm without a compass, each day presenting a new test of our collective resolve. Their sorrow, a tempest of varied expressions, became the most poignant challenge we faced as a family, reshaping our understanding of resilience, grace, and the healing power of empathy.

Witnessing their struggle, feeling the raw edges of their pain alongside them, demanded more than perseverance. It called for a deep well of grace — for Jack and John, as they navigated the uncharted territories of loss; for ourselves, as we endeavored to be their beacon and shelter in the midst of their storm; and for the memory of Mike, whose absence was a constant presence in our lives, a silent witness to the complex tapestry of emotions we were attempting to weave into a new form of family unity.

This journey through their grief taught us that grace is not merely the act of forgiveness or a passive state of acceptance. It is an active, powerful force that empowers us to face the most daunting challenges with compassion and strength. Offering grace to Jack and John meant acknowledging their pain without judgment, validating their emotions, and providing a steadfast presence they could rely on, even in their darkest moments. It involved countless conversations, where words were often inadequate but presence spoke volumes, and actions, no matter how small, conveyed the depth of our commitment to their healing.

Similarly, extending grace to ourselves was a crucial, albeit challenging, aspect of this journey. It required us to forgive our own moments of doubt and frustration, to recognize that our capacity to support Jack and John was intertwined with our own need for self-care and healing. It was a delicate balancing act, where the acknowledgment of our limitations became as important as our efforts to push beyond them.

Grace for Mike's memory, meanwhile, involved a process of reconciliation with the past, an attempt to understand the complexities of his life and the decisions that led to his suicide. It was a journey through our own feelings of anger, betrayal, and sorrow, towards a place of empathy and, ultimately, peace. This aspect of grace was perhaps the most complex, as it challenged us to look beyond our immediate pain and embrace a broader perspective on the human experience, with all its flaws and frailties.

The emotional tumult of Jack and John's grief, with its myriad expressions, tested our resolve in ways we could never have anticipated. Yet, it was through this very challenge that we discovered the true strength of our family. In offering grace to each other, we found a resilience that was not just about enduring but about transforming — turning pain into empathy, despair into hope, and a family forged from loss into a testament to the enduring power of love and understanding. This journey, though fraught with challenges, has illuminated the depth of our capacity for grace, resilience, and the healing that comes from truly walking together through the storm.

Navigating the emotional upheavals of Jack and John was akin to walking through a constantly shifting landscape, where the terrain of grief could alter from impassable mountains of anger to deep valleys of despair without warning. This journey taught us the delicate art of holding space for their pain—a concept that, before now, was more theoretical than practical in our lives. It demanded of us a patience and understanding that stretched the very fabric of our being, testing our resolve and the depth of our compassion.

There were days when the boys' grief manifested as storms of rage, their words sharp as lightning, striking at the heart of our family's fragile peace. These outbursts, though frightening in their intensity, were expressions of the deep-seated pain and confusion that churned within them. On other days, their sorrow would cloak them in silence, a dense fog that isolated them from our attempts to reach out and connect. Witnessing their struggle, feeling the raw edges of their pain alongside them, was a profound challenge. It required us to summon a resilience that went beyond mere perseverance, calling on us to tap into a deep well of grace—not just for the boys but for ourselves, as we navigated the complex terrain of guardianship and healing.

This process, inevitably, was fraught with missteps. Our patience, though steadfast, was not inexhaustible. There were moments when the enormity of our responsibilities, the depth of the boys' grief, and the lingering pain of our own losses frayed the edges of our composure. Misunderstandings and frustrations, on occasion, boiled over into heated exchanges, leaving a trail of regret and sorrow in their wake.

Yet, it was precisely in these moments of vulnerability and apparent failure that grace revealed its transformative power. Apologies, soft and sincere, became the balm that soothed the wounds of our conflicts. Shared tears in the quiet of the night served as silent testimonies of our shared burden and mutual love. These instances of grace—both given and received—became our compass, guiding us back to one another, reinforcing the bonds that grief had threatened to unravel.

Grace, in its most profound essence, became the light that illuminated our path through the darkness. It taught us that holding space for grief was not merely about providing a physical presence but about offering an emotional sanctuary—a place where anger could be expressed, tears could be shed, and silence could be respected without judgment. This journey of understanding and acceptance was not linear nor free from obstacles, but it was paved with countless moments of grace that drew us closer, deepening our connection and reinforcing the love that united us as a family. Through grace, we found our way back to each other, time and again, fortified by the knowledge that, together, we could weather the tempests of grief and emerge, not unscathed, but stronger and more connected than ever before.

Our family's narrative, intricately woven with threads of loss, love, and resilience, was deeply marked by our relationship with Mike. His final act, leaving behind a wake of unanswered questions and profound grief, plunged us into a maelstrom of emotions that tested the very essence of our bond and beliefs. Confronting our feelings towards him, we embarked on a journey that was as much about understanding and forgiveness as it was about healing and acceptance.

In the initial aftermath of Mike's suicide, our emotions were a tangled web of anger, sorrow, and confusion. Anger, for the pain he inflicted upon Jack and John sorrow, for the myriad of struggles he must have faced in silence; and confusion, over how such a decision could have been seen as the only recourse. These emotions, raw and unyielding, threatened to overshadow the memories of the man Mike once was—a brother, a father, a friend.

The process of untangling these emotions was neither swift nor straightforward. It demanded of us a profound level of introspection and empathy, pushing us to delve into the complexities of Mike's life and the battles he fought in the shadows. Through countless conversations, often steeped in tears and whispers of what could have been, we sought to piece together the fragments of his story, to find some semblance of understanding amidst the chaos of our grief.

This endeavor to understand Mike was not an attempt to excuse his actions but rather to view them through a lens of compassion. It was a recognition of the harsh truth that mental illness and despair do not discriminate, that they can ensnare even the most seemingly strong individuals in their grip. By acknowledging his struggles, we began to dismantle the wall of judgment that had risen between us, allowing us to see him not just as the architect of his fate but as a victim of his circumstances.

Finding grace in this context was akin to navigating through darkness with only a flicker of light as guidance. Grace became our beacon, illuminating the path towards forgiveness and understanding. It taught us that forgiveness was not a sign of weakness but a powerful act of liberation—from the chains of anger, from the dungeons of resentment, and from the cycle of pain that threatened to consume us.

Forgiving Mike, however, was only one facet of our journey. Equally challenging was the task of forgiving ourselves. Guilt, a silent specter, often haunted our thoughts—guilt for not having seen the signs, for not having reached out more, for the myriad of what-ifs that lingered like ghosts in the aftermath of his departure. Through grace, we learned to extend the same compassion we sought for Mike towards ourselves. We came to understand that forgiveness was a gift we owed not just to him but to ourselves, a crucial step in unburdening our hearts and paving the way for true healing.

This journey of understanding and forgiveness, facilitated by grace, was transformative. It allowed us to view Mike's actions and our own responses through a more compassionate lens, fostering a deeper sense of empathy within ourselves. It taught us the invaluable lesson that grace is not just about extending forgiveness to others but also about embracing our vulnerabilities and imperfections with kindness and understanding.

Nest Refilled:
A Journey of Grit, Grace, and Renewal

As we moved forward, the shadow of Mike's choices remained a part of our story, but it no longer defined us. Instead, our journey through the darkness, guided by the light of grace, became a testament to our family's resilience and capacity for healing. It underscored the profound power of grace to heal the deepest of wounds, to bridge the widest of divides, and to light the way through the darkest of nights.

Through grace, we found the strength to release the anchor of unresolved bitterness, allowing us to navigate the tumultuous waters of grief with a newfound sense of peace and purpose. Our journey taught us that while forgiveness does not erase the past, it opens the door to a future where love and understanding can flourish, free from the chains of resentment. It was a journey marked by pain, but more importantly, by the redemptive power of grace—a journey that, though born from loss, led us to a deeper understanding of ourselves, each other, and the capacity of the human heart to heal and to forgive.

In the journey of weaving the new fabric of our family, we found ourselves navigating not just the internal dynamics of grief, healing, and adaptation but also the external landscape marked by societal judgments. The world outside our unit, with its propensity for categorization, often viewed our unconventional family structure through a lens of skepticism and curiosity. Whispers at school functions, stares in grocery store aisles, and the sometimes-outright questions about the nature of our relationship to Jack and John underscored a pervasive discomfort with the reality of our existence—a reality that defied traditional norms and expectations.

This external scrutiny tested our collective resolve, challenging us to maintain our unity and dignity in the face of unwarranted judgment. It was a scenario that demanded not just grit to withstand the pressures but also grace to navigate these interactions with poise and understanding. Rather than retreating into defensiveness, we chose to engage, transforming these moments of judgment into opportunities for advocacy and education.

Our response to societal curiosity and skepticism was rooted in openness and honesty. We shared our story not as a means to justify our family's legitimacy but as an invitation to broaden the perspective on what constitutes a family. Each query, whether veiled in politeness or brimming with prejudice, was met with a narrative of love, resilience, and commitment—a narrative that highlighted the diverse forms love and family can take.

This proactive approach did more than fortify our internal resolve; it became a means to chip away at the barriers of misunderstanding and prejudice that often divide communities. By sharing our experiences, we not only advocated for families like ours but also illuminated the common threads of humanity that bind us all—love, loss, and the universal quest for belonging and understanding.

Moreover, engaging with the community, whether through formal platforms such as speaking engagements and workshops or through informal conversations, allowed us to present our family as a testament to the transformative power of love and acceptance. We highlighted the journey of Jack and John, showcasing their resilience and the depth of their characters, which had flourished in the nurturing environment of our unconventional family. These narratives, shared with vulnerability and pride, served as powerful antidotes to prejudice, demonstrating the capacity of non-traditional families to provide the same foundation of love, security, and growth as their traditional counterparts.

Our interactions with the wider community also revealed allies in unexpected places. Teachers, neighbors, and even strangers, moved by our story, offered support and solidarity, reinforcing the notion that the essence of family transcends societal constructs. These connections, forged in the shared recognition of our common humanity, underscored the importance of dialogue in breaking down barriers and fostering a more inclusive understanding of family dynamics.

The journey of responding to societal judgments with grace and advocacy was not without its challenges. There were moments of frustration, of feeling misunderstood or undervalued by the very society we were a part of. Yet, it was in these moments that the lessons of our internal journey—of forgiveness, understanding, and resilience—proved invaluable. They reminded us that the power to define our family's worth and legitimacy lay not in societal approval but in the strength of our bonds and the authenticity of our love.

As we navigated the complexities of our external environment, the very act of living our truth became a form of advocacy. Our family, in its daily existence and interactions, stood as a living challenge to narrow definitions of love and family, encouraging a broader, more inclusive perspective. This approach not only contributed to our sense of empowerment but also inspired others to question and expand their understanding of what it means to be a family.

Looking back through the shadows of societal judgments, we recognize that each challenge faced and each barrier overcome has enriched our family's tapestry. It has taught us the value of grit in standing firm in our identity and the transformative power of grace in turning challenges into opportunities for growth and understanding. Through our story, shared with openness and honesty, we hope to contribute to a more compassionate, inclusive world where families of all forms are recognized for the love that binds them, free from the constraints of conventional labels and prejudices.

Meditating on these moments of grit and grace in action, it becomes clear that they are not just challenges to be overcome but essential parts of our growth as individuals and as a family. They taught us the strength inherent in vulnerability, the beauty of forgiveness, and the transformative power of compassion. These lessons, hard-earned and deeply felt, have not only helped us navigate the complexities of our journey but have also imbued us with a profound sense of gratitude for the journey itself. Through this lens, we have come to understand that it is not the absence of challenges that defines us, but the way we rise to meet them, together.

Chapter 5: Finding a New Rhythm

In the wake of upheaval and change, our family embarked on a quest not just for stability but for a new rhythm that would define our collective existence. This journey, marked by trials and triumphs, was a testament to our resilience and the unyielding power of love to forge paths through the wilderness of the unknown.

In the midst of the upheaval that reshaped our lives, establishing new routines emerged as the bedrock upon which we began to construct our new normal. This endeavor, far from a mere organizational task, became a critical component of our healing process and a means to foster a sense of security and belonging for Jack and John. The chaos that once defined our existence gradually gave way to a structured harmony, punctuated by the daily rituals that we came to cherish.

Morning breakfasts, previously rushed and often neglected amidst the turmoil of early days, were reimagined into moments of connection and reflection. We transformed these early hours into a time of intentionality, where the act of breaking bread together became a shared ritual. It was here that we shared our hopes for the day ahead, discussed upcoming events, and sometimes, ventured into deeper territories of dreams and fears. This ritual, simple in its execution, became a cornerstone of our daily life, setting the tone for the day and reinforcing our commitment to navigate this journey together.

Evenings, too, took on a new significance. The end of each day brought us back together, a reconvening of hearts and minds in the familial space we were learning to navigate. These gatherings were not mandated but naturally evolved as a time to decompress, share, and support one another. Whether it was through assisting with homework, which often became a learning experience for all involved, or discussing the events of our days, these moments were imbued with a sense of purpose. On some nights, we would forego conversations for the shared silence of reading or the communal laughter brought on by a family movie. The variety of our evening activities reflected the diversity of our needs and personalities, yet each served the same essential purpose: to reinforce the bonds of our burgeoning family unit.

The establishment of these routines did more than just provide structure; they became sacred rituals that anchored us in a sea of uncertainty. The predictability of our daily activities offered a contrast to the unpredictability of our emotions, providing a comforting rhythm in the background of our lives. More importantly, these rituals became acts of care, tangible expressions of our commitment to one another's well-being and happiness.

As we settled into these routines, we noticed a gradual shift in the atmosphere of our home. The initial tension and awkwardness that accompanied our interactions began to dissipate, replaced by a warmth and familiarity that spoke of deeper connections. Jack and John, once hesitant participants in these rituals, started to bring their own ideas and preferences into our planning, signaling a growing sense of ownership and belonging within the family. Their engagement was a clear indicator of the trust and comfort they were beginning to feel, a testament to the power of consistency and shared experiences in building a family.

Yet, the process of establishing these routines was not without its challenges. Balancing the individual needs of each family member with the collective goals of our unit required flexibility and patience. There were days when the best-laid plans unraveled, when the strain of homework led to frustration rather than bonding, or when the simple act of gathering for breakfast felt like a Herculean effort. These moments tested our resolve but also taught us valuable lessons in adaptability and forgiveness. We learned that routines, while important, needed to allow space for spontaneity and grace. It was okay to deviate from the plan, to forego an evening activity in favor of quiet reflection or impromptu ice cream runs.

In reflecting on the journey of establishing our new routines, it's evident that these structured daily activities served as more than just anchors; they were the loom upon which we wove the fabric of our new life together. Each thread, representing a shared meal, a conversation, or a moment of laughter, contributed to the creation of a family tapestry rich with the colors of love, understanding, and mutual respect. Through the intentional design of our days, we found not just stability but a deeper sense of connection and belonging. Our routines, mundane as they might initially appear, became the sacred rituals that defined us, offering comfort, predictability, and, most importantly, a foundation upon which we could build our future together.

Amidst the tumult that reshaped our lives, finding grounding in the form of routines became not just a method of coping, but a vital strategy for building the new framework of our family life. This shift from disarray to structure was neither quick nor effortless, but it was imbued with a profound sense of purpose and intentionality. As we navigated this transformation, the establishment of daily routines emerged as a cornerstone of our new normal, anchoring us amidst the fluctuating tides of grief and adjustment.

Evenings, too, were deliberately structured to reinforce this sense of unity and belonging. Reserved for family time, these hours became a canvas upon which we painted the moments of our collective life. Some evenings were dedicated to academic support, where homework sessions served dual purposes: addressing educational needs and providing a deeper understanding of each other's strengths and challenges. Other times, we engaged in discussions about the day's events, which often veered into broader conversations about life, dreams, and occasionally, the memories of those we had lost. These discussions, rich with emotion and insight, were instrumental in fostering a deeper connection among us.

Yet, it wasn't just the deep conversations or the academic activities that defined our evenings. Simple acts of being together, whether through watching a movie, playing a board game, or just sitting in comfortable silence, became just as meaningful. These moments, mundane on the surface, were layered with significance, reinforcing our bond and providing a sense of security and togetherness.

The transition to these new routines was not without its challenges. Initially, the attempt to instill structure was met with resistance, especially from Jack and John, who were navigating their own turbulent seas of emotion. The shift from what was to what could be required patience, understanding, and a willingness to adapt. Missteps were inevitable, but they provided valuable lessons in the importance of flexibility and the need to tailor our routines to fit the changing contours of our family life.

One of the most significant realizations in this journey was the understanding that routines, while structured, needed to breathe. They had to be flexible enough to accommodate the unexpected moments that life invariably presents. This understanding led us to approach our routines with a sense of fluidity, allowing us to adjust and adapt as necessary. It was in this space of flexibility that we found our most meaningful moments of connection and growth.

Moreover, the establishment of these routines did more than provide a semblance of normalcy; they became a vehicle for healing. The predictability and security afforded by our structured daily activities offered Jack and John a foundation upon which they could begin to process their grief and rebuild their sense of self within the safety of our family unit. For us as guardians, these routines provided a way to demonstrate our love and commitment, reinforcing the message that, despite the upheaval, we were a family, connected by bonds stronger than blood.

In crafting our new normal through the establishment of routines, we wove a fabric of continuity and care that enveloped our family. These routines, seemingly mundane, emerged as sacred rituals that marked the passage of our days, imbuing them with meaning and purpose. They allowed us to carve out a space of stability in an otherwise uncertain world, offering comfort and predictability in the midst of change.

As we reflect on the journey of establishing our new routines, it's clear that this process was instrumental in shaping the identity of our family. It facilitated a deeper understanding of each other's needs, provided a framework for support and connection, and, most importantly, it helped us find joy in the simple act of being together. Through the intentional creation of these daily rituals, we not only found our new rhythm but also discovered the enduring strength and resilience of our family bond.

In the evolving narrative of our family, the cultivation of traditions became a cornerstone of our identity, a way to weave the unique threads of our individual pasts into a collective tapestry that spoke of unity, resilience, and hope. As we navigated the complexities of blending our lives, the intentional creation and adaptation of traditions served not just as reminders of our journey but as anchors in the fluid seas of change.

Birthdays and holidays, those universal markers of time and milestones of personal significance, took on a deeper resonance within the framework of our new family dynamic. We approached these occasions with a blend of reverence for the past and a creative eye towards the future, seeking to honor the memories and customs that Jack and John brought with them while infusing these celebrations with new meaning. This delicate balance allowed us to acknowledge the loss and absence that underscored our existence, while also celebrating the love and connection that now defined us. Birthday celebrations, for example, transformed from simple gatherings into layered events that combined favorite meals from our pasts with new rituals, such as planting a tree or crafting a piece of art together—acts that symbolized growth, continuity, and the nurturing of new life from the soil of old memories.

The adaptation of holiday traditions also played a pivotal role in our collective healing and bonding. Recognizing that holidays could evoke a profound sense of loss and nostalgia for Jack and John, we approached these times with sensitivity and inclusivity. We invited the boys to share their most cherished holiday memories and rituals, which we then incorporated into our celebrations. This inclusion not only validated their feelings and past experiences but also helped bridge the gap between old and new, weaving their history into the fabric of our shared present. In turn, we introduced new customs, such as a gratitude circle on Thanksgiving, where each of us would share what we were thankful for, including the challenges that taught us resilience and the moments of joy that gave us hope. These practices, though simple, became profound declarations of our family's values and our commitment to one another.

Moreover, the establishment of entirely new traditions became a way for us to chart our course, to create markers of our journey that were uniquely ours. The Sunday jollof rice ritual, for instance, became a weekly celebration of togetherness, a time when the kitchen buzzed with activity and laughter, and the air was thick with the aroma of puff-puff. These moments, though ordinary in their execution, were extraordinary in their ability to foster a sense of belonging and joy. Similarly, the annual family hike to commemorate the start of spring became a metaphor for our journey—each step a reminder of the obstacles we'd overcome and the distances we'd traversed together, both literally and metaphorically.

Through the cultivation of these traditions, we found not only comfort and joy but also a profound sense of identity. They became the milestones that marked our progress, the rituals that bound us together, and the memories that would define our legacy. In the process of creating and adapting these traditions, we discovered the true essence of family: not a static entity defined by convention but a dynamic, living organism, nurtured by the shared experiences and the love that flows between its members.

As we look back on the traditions that have come to define us, it's clear that their value lies not in the rituals themselves but in what they represent: the resilience to adapt, the courage to embrace change, and the love that sustains us through it all. These traditions, both old and new, stand as testaments to our family's journey, celebrating where we've come from, who we are now, and the endless possibilities of what we can become together.

In the journey of redefining our family, amidst the backdrop of challenge and change, the cultivation of joy emerged not merely as an unexpected gift but as a vital pillar of our daily existence. The initial days of our union were often shadowed by the heaviness of loss and the daunting task of adjustment, where moments of joy seemed as fleeting and rare as shafts of light through overcast skies. Yet, it was in these very flashes of happiness that we found the strength and inspiration to seek out and nurture joy with deliberate intention.

The transformation began subtly, rooted in the recognition that joy need not be grandiose or planned, but could be found in the simplest of moments, often when least expected. A spontaneous game of tag in the backyard, initially embarked upon to dispel the afternoon's ennui, turned into a riotous expedition of laughter and playful competition. The sight of Jack and John, usually so guarded, letting go of their burdens long enough to simply be kids, was a heartening reminder of the resilience of youth and the healing power of play. Similarly, an impromptu dance party in the living room, sparked by a favorite song playing on the radio, saw us shedding our inhibitions along with our shoes, as we danced away the day's worries in a shared celebration of the moment.

These instances of joy, while simple, carried profound significance. They served as reminders that even in the midst of sorrow and upheaval, life could still offer moments of unadulterated happiness. More importantly, they underscored the fact that joy was not just a fleeting emotion but a state of being that could be cultivated and cherished. As we became more attuned to each other and the rhythms of our new life together, the search for these moments of joy shifted from a passive hope to an active pursuit.

This pursuit of joy also became a means of strengthening our bonds with each other. Shared laughter over a silly joke at the dinner table, or the collective satisfaction of completing a puzzle on a rainy afternoon, became the threads that wove our experiences together, creating a tapestry rich with the colors of shared happiness. These moments, no matter how brief, became the milestones by which we measured our progress, not just as individuals but as a family unit.

Moreover, the intentional embrace of joy taught us valuable lessons about the nature of happiness itself. We learned that joy does not negate the presence of sorrow or struggle; rather, it coexists with them, offering balance and perspective. It taught us that happiness is not a destination to be reached but a journey to be experienced, marked by moments that lift the heart and spirit.

As we reflect on the journey of finding and nurturing moments of joy within our family, it becomes clear that these instances have been more than just breaks in the cloud cover of our collective challenges. They have been the light that guided us through, illuminating our path forward and warming the soil from which our new life together has grown. These moments of joy, once fleeting and rare, have become the undercurrent of our existence, a testament to our ability to find happiness in the here and now, and a reminder of the enduring capacity for joy that resides within each of us.

In embracing these moments with intentionality, we have not only enriched our daily lives but have also laid the foundation for a family culture that values joy, resilience, and the power of shared experiences. This culture, rooted in the simple yet profound moments of happiness we've shared, stands as a beacon of hope and a testament to the enduring strength and love that defines our family.

The journey toward solidifying our bond as a newly formed family was akin to charting a course through unexplored territories, each step informed by a blend of intuition, love, and the collective will to emerge stronger on the other side. This path, while punctuated with the inherent challenges of blending lives and healing from past wounds, was rich with opportunities for growth and deepening connections. It was through the establishment of our daily routines, the cultivation of cherished traditions, and the embrace of spontaneous moments of joy that the essence of our family began to crystallize, revealing the depth of our commitment and the strength of our collective spirit.

The daily routines we established served as the scaffolding for our evolving family structure, providing a sense of predictability and security that was previously absent. Morning gatherings around the breakfast table and evening discussions became more than just bookends to our days; they were vital channels through which we communicated our hopes, fears, and aspirations. These routines, while simple in execution, were profound in their impact, offering a steady rhythm to our lives and fostering an environment where each voice could be heard and valued.

Simultaneously, the traditions we nurtured became the landmarks of our journey, signifying our progress and celebrating our unity. From the joyous cacophony of our Saturday morning pancake rituals to the reflective tranquility of our annual spring hikes, these traditions wove a rich tapestry of shared experiences that underscored our identity as a family. They served as reminders of our journey from a collection of individuals navigating the aftermath of loss and change to a cohesive unit bound by a deep sense of belonging and purpose.

Moreover, it was in the spontaneous moments of joy—those unplanned instances of laughter and light-heartedness—that the true essence of our bond was revealed. Whether it was an impromptu game of tag that dissolved into fits of laughter or a collectively cooked meal that turned the kitchen into a scene of delightful chaos, these moments underscored the capacity for joy and resilience that lay at the heart of our family. They reminded us that amidst the challenges and routines of daily life, there was always space for the unexpected sparks of happiness that could bring us closer together.

This journey of adjustment, discovery, and celebration was instrumental in solidifying our bond. Each routine established, tradition embraced, and moment of joy shared contributed to a deeper understanding of one another, revealing the multifaceted dimensions of our characters and the depths of our resilience. Through these shared experiences, we learned the invaluable lesson that our strength as a family did not reside in the absence of challenges but in our collective ability to face them with grace, understanding, and an unwavering commitment to each other.

As we reflect on the significance of finding our new rhythm, it becomes apparent that this process was transformative, not just in the context of adapting to our changed circumstances but in the profound ways it reshaped our understanding of family and belonging. Our new rhythm, unique to us, emerged as a testament to our journey—a melody rich with the nuances of our shared experiences and the harmony of our combined strengths. It became our anthem, symbolizing not just our resilience in the face of adversity but also our capacity for joy, love, and hopeful anticipation of the future.

Moving forward, the rhythm we have found serves not as a rigid structure to which we must conform but as a fluid harmony that adapts to the ebb and flow of our lives. It speaks to who we have become together—a family defined not by conventional standards but by the richness of our shared experiences, the depth of our understanding, and the joy we find in each new day together. This rhythm, while uniquely ours, resonates with the universal themes of love, resilience, and the endless potential for transformation, serving as a beacon of hope and a source of strength as we continue our journey together.

Chapter 6: Lessons in Love and Loss

Our journey, marked by the intertwining paths of grief and growth, has unfolded lessons about the depths of human emotion, the resilience required to navigate loss, and the boundless capacity of love to heal and transform. In traversing this landscape, we've encountered revelations about love's multifaceted nature, the complexities of loss, and the intricate process of healing—particularly through the lens of forgiving Mike.

Our odyssey through the complexities of forming a new family amidst the backdrop of profound loss has been a conduit for deep, often surprising, lessons about the human condition. This journey, interwoven with the threads of grief and the vibrant hues of growth, has illuminated the multifaceted nature of love, the labyrinthine pathways of loss, and the transformative potential of healing. Central to this narrative has been the arduous process of coming to terms with, and ultimately forgiving, Mike for the waves of disruption his actions sent through our lives.

Our journey, deeply etched with the complexities of blending lives amidst the echoes of loss, has been a profound exploration into the myriad forms of love. Far beyond the realms of the romantic or the familial ties by blood, we discovered love as a dynamic, transformative force—a catalyst for healing, a binder of fragmented pieces, and a beacon guiding us through the darkest valleys. This multifaceted experience of love has broadened our understanding, teaching us about its capacity for patience, its foundation in empathy, and the inherent courage it demands to fully embrace each other, complete with our shadows and light.

Nest Refilled:
A Journey of Grit, Grace, and Renewal

Patience emerged as one of love's most challenging aspects, particularly in the early stages of our journey. Integrating Jack and John into our lives, and navigating the tumult of emotions that swirled around us, required a patience that was both tender and tenacious. This patience was not merely about waiting for time to heal the wounds but actively holding space for each other's pain, allowing each member the time they needed to adjust, to grieve, and to find their footing in this new reality we were constructing together. It was patience that allowed us to approach each setback not as a failure but as a part of the process, understanding that healing and bonding take time and cannot be rushed.

Empathy, the ability to truly understand and share the feelings of another, became the cornerstone of our expanding notion of love. It was empathy that enabled us to see the world through Jack and John 's eyes—to feel the depth of their loss, the disorientation of their new circumstances, and the bravery with which they faced each day. This empathy bridged gaps between us, fostering a deep, compassionate connection that went beyond mere sympathy. It taught us to listen not just with our ears but with our hearts, to recognize the unspoken fears and hopes that lingered Beneath the surface. Empathy allowed us to connect on a level where words were unnecessary, where simply being present offered comfort and understanding.

Perhaps the most surprising lesson was learning about the courage inherent in love. It took courage to open our hearts to Jack and John, knowing the potential for future loss and pain. It required bravery to confront our own vulnerabilities and to extend trust again, especially in the shadow of Mike's suicide. This courage was manifest in our willingness to embrace each other in our entirety, accepting not only the bright aspects of our personalities but also the darker, more challenging facets. It was a courage that said, "I see you, all of you, and I choose to love you still." This form of love—fierce, unflinching, and unconditional—became the glue that held us together, allowing us to rebuild from the ruins of our respective pasts into something stronger and more beautiful.

Central to our understanding of love's many forms was the realization that its truest test and greatest strength lie in the ability to walk together through the valley of loss. Love, in this context, became an act of mutual support and shared resilience, a commitment to hold onto each other even when the path forward was shrouded in the fog of grief. It was in the shared moments of vulnerability, in the collective courage to face each day, that the depth and strength of our love were fully revealed. These moments, though fraught with pain, became milestones of our collective journey, teaching us that love, in its essence, is not diminished by hardship but is instead forged and deepened by it.

The journey of understanding love's many forms has been, at its core, a process of reconstruction. From the fragmented pieces of our individual and collective experiences, we have built a family bound by a love that is expansive, inclusive, and profoundly healing. This love has not only guided us through the challenges we've faced but has also illuminated the path forward, showing us the potential for joy, connection, and growth even in the aftermath of profound loss.

As we continue to navigate the waters of this journey, our expanded understanding of love stands as a testament to our resilience and our capacity for transformation. It reaffirms the belief that love, in all its forms, is the most powerful force we have for healing, for binding us together, and for transforming the deepest wounds into sources of strength and beauty. This love, complex and multifaceted, is our anthem and our anchor, guiding us toward a future where the music of our shared experiences continues to play, richer and more nuanced for the journey we have undertaken together.

The landscape of loss is rugged, uncharted, and profoundly personal, yet it's a terrain that our family has traversed together, each step revealing the complexities and transformative power of grief. The loss of Mike cast long shadows across our lives, initiating a journey through the labyrinth of sorrow, where the echoes of what was and the silence of what will never be again intertwine. This voyage through the valley of loss, while laden with heartache, has also unfolded invaluable lessons about the essence of human existence, the impermanence that underscores our lives, and the resilience that propels us forward.

Confronting loss forced us to face the fragility of life head-on. It was a stark reminder that existence is fleeting, a transient whisper between the eternities of the unknown. This harsh truth, though difficult to accept, fostered a profound appreciation for the present moment and the importance of cherishing the time we have with those we love. It taught us to live more intentionally, to embrace each day with gratitude, and to not take the presence of one another for granted. In this way, loss, with its cruel sharpness, also served as a clarion call to value and celebrate the beauty of the now, to make space for joy and love amidst the sorrow.

Through Jack and John's journey with grief, we witnessed the transformative impact of loss on the soul. Their sorrow, a palpable entity, seemed at times too vast to navigate. Yet, as we moved through the days and months, this grief began to carve out new depths within them, and indeed within us all. These spaces of sorrow became reservoirs for a deeper understanding of life and our connections to each other. Loss taught us empathy in its purest form, the ability to stand in the shadow of another's pain and offer solace not through words, but through the simple act of being present. It reshaped our perspectives, revealing that within the heart of loss lie seeds of growth, understanding, and an enhanced capacity for love.

Navigating the complexities of loss has also been an exercise in finding light in the darkest of times. This search for light was not about denying the pain or the reality of our grief but about seeking moments of hope, beauty, and connection that exist alongside sorrow. It was in the laughter shared over a memory of Mike, in the healing found in tears shed together, and in the solace discovered in shared silence. These moments, though fleeting, illuminated our path through grief, reminding us that darkness does not extinguish light but makes it all the more precious. They taught us resilience—the art of carrying forward despite the weight of loss, of holding onto hope even when it feels tenuous at best.

Perhaps one of the most profound lessons gleaned from our journey with loss is the importance of carrying forward the legacies of those we've lost. Mike's absence left a void, but it also left us with memories, lessons, and love that continue to shape our lives. In honoring his memory, in speaking his name and sharing stories of his life, we found a way to keep his spirit alive within the fabric of our family. This act of remembrance became a testament to the enduring impact of love and the belief that those we've loved and lost continue to walk with us, woven into the stories of who we are and who we aspire to be.

Coping with the intricacies of grief has been a journey marked by tears, reflection, and ultimately, growth. It has shown us that grief, while a universal experience, is uniquely personal in its impact and lessons. Through this journey, we've learned that loss, in all its pain and sorrow, also holds the potential for profound transformation—shaping us into individuals and a family marked by deeper empathy, resilience, and an unwavering commitment to cherish and celebrate the moments we have together. In embracing the lessons of loss, we find the strength to move forward, carrying with us the memories and legacies of those we've loved, allowing them to illuminate our path toward healing and hope.

The journey of healing, with its intricate web of emotions and revelations, has been a pivotal aspect of our family's narrative, especially in the context of grappling with Mike's departure. For me, this process was not just about navigating the tumultuous waters of grief but also about confronting the deep-seated feelings of betrayal and abandonment left in the wake of his actions. This journey toward forgiveness and healing illuminated the multifaceted nature of the healing process itself—a journey that is neither linear nor predictable but rich with opportunities for profound personal growth and understanding.

My initial encounter with the concept of forgiving Mike was marked by resistance. The complexity of my emotions—anger at his departure, despair over the loss it represented, and confusion about the future—created a tumultuous inner landscape that seemed insurmountable. Forgiveness, in these early stages, appeared as an elusive, perhaps even undesirable, goal. The betrayal I felt, compounded by the responsibility to shepherd Jack and John through their grief, felt like chains binding me to a past I wished to forget but could not escape.

Yet, amidst the storm of emotions, there were moments of unexpected clarity—instances where the anger and despair gave way to insights into the human condition and the universality of suffering. These revelations began to soften the hard edges of my resentment, suggesting that Mike's actions, though unfathomable, were born out of his own profound struggle. It was in these moments that the seeds of empathy were sown, allowing me to view Mike not just as the source of my pain but as a fellow traveler on life's difficult journey, burdened with his own share of torment.

The path to forgiveness necessitated a deep, often painful, exploration of my heart. It required me to peel back the layers of pain, to confront the raw wounds left by Mike's departure, and to acknowledge my vulnerabilities. This process was far from easy; it was a journey marked by setbacks and moments of doubt. Yet, it was also a journey illuminated by moments of profound insight and growth. As I delved deeper into my process of healing, I discovered that forgiveness was not about absolving Mike of responsibility but about releasing myself from the burden of ongoing resentment and anger.

Gradually, my journey led me to a place of empathy for Mike—a realization that his actions, while deeply hurtful, were not born out of malice but from a place of despair and isolation. This understanding did not erase the pain of his loss but allowed me to view him with a compassion that had previously seemed impossible. Empathy became the bridge that connected my experiences of pain to Mike's, revealing the shared human vulnerability that underlies all acts of desperation.

Ultimately, I found that forgiving Mike was intrinsically linked to my healing journey. Forgiveness became a release—a way to cut the chains of bitterness and to step forward into a future unburdened by the weight of past grievances. This act of forgiveness did not happen overnight; it was the culmination of a long, often arduous process. Yet, it was a step that brought with it a sense of peace and closure, not just for me but for our entire family. It allowed us to move forward, not by forgetting the past but by embracing the lessons and strength we had gained from it.

The healing process, as my journey has shown, is deeply intertwined with the ability to forgive—not just others but ourselves as well. It's a process that teaches us about the resilience of the human spirit, the capacity for empathy and understanding, and the transformative power of compassion. Through forgiveness, we find a way to transcend the pain of loss and betrayal, to rediscover the strength and love that bind us together as a family, and to open our hearts to the possibility of a future shaped not by grief but by the lessons of love and loss we have learned along the way.

Forgiveness, in its essence, is an act of profound courage and compassion, a theme poignantly illustrated in my journey toward forgiving Mike. This path was neither straightforward nor devoid of pain; it was a nuanced exploration of the depths of human emotion and the capacity to transcend personal hurt in search of peace. My decision to forgive emerged from a complex tapestry of love, loss, and the longing for resolution—not just for me but for the entire fabric of our newly formed family, especially for Jack and John, who were navigating their own mazes of grief.

Forgiveness, as I discovered, is multifaceted. It is not about condoning actions or forgetting the hurt they've caused but about freeing oneself from the perpetual cycle of anger and bitterness. This understanding began to take root as I delved into the complexities of Mike's life, his struggles, and the despair that ultimately led to his tragic decision. Viewing him through this lens of empathy and understanding did not diminish the impact of his actions but allowed for a broader perspective on the human condition—one marked by vulnerability, pain, and the capacity for error.

The shift in perspective was gradual, an unfolding that occurred over countless moments of reflection, dialogue, and, importantly, moments of silence. It involved re-evaluating the narrative that had been constructed around Mike's departure, one that had, understandably, been tinged with anger and confusion. By acknowledging his complexities as an individual—his battles with mental health, his moments of joy and despair—I began to see him not just as the source of their pain but as someone who was deeply pained himself. This re-contextualization was crucial, acting as a bridge from a place of resentment to one of understanding and compassion.

This journey towards forgiveness was intrinsically linked to the healing process. The act of releasing Mike from the confines of anger and resentment did not negate the reality of the pain he caused but opened a pathway to healing that was blocked by the harboring of negative emotions. For my, and by extension, our family, forgiveness became a conduit for peace—a peace not predicated on the erasure of past hurt but on the understanding and acceptance of its complexities. It allowed us to honor our feelings of loss and betrayal while also making room for compassion and empathy, illuminating the way forward.

The effects of my forgiveness extended beyond her individual healing, touching the lives of Jack, John, and the cohesive unit we were striving to become. It demonstrated the power of forgiveness to transform not only the individual who forgives but also the environment around them. In choosing forgiveness, I set an example of strength, compassion, and the importance of seeking peace over clinging to pain. This act of forgiveness became a cornerstone of our family's narrative, a testament to the idea that from the depths of despair and hurt can emerge an opportunity for growth, understanding, and a deeper connection to each other.

It's crucial to recognize that forgiveness is not a one-time act but an ongoing journey, a continuous choice to lean towards understanding and peace. For me, and indeed for each of us, the decision to forgive Mike is revisited and reaffirmed through the challenges and reminders of his absence. It's a path marked by its share of obstacles, moments of doubt, and resurgence of grief. Yet, it's also a journey illuminated by the light of compassion, understanding, and the profound realization that forgiveness is one of the most powerful forms of love—a love that heals, transforms, and leads us toward peace.

In embracing forgiveness as a path to peace, our family has discovered not just the capacity to overcome the pain of the past but also the resilience and compassion to build a future grounded in understanding and love. This journey has taught us that while forgiveness may not change the past, it has the power to transform the future, offering a foundation of peace and healing upon which we can continue to grow and thrive together.

The journey our family has embarked upon, marked by the intertwining of profound loss and the gradual weaving of new bonds, has unfolded a rich tapestry of lessons that speak to the very essence of what it means to be human. Reflecting on these lessons reveals a landscape of emotion and experience that underscores the indomitable resilience of the human spirit and the boundless capacity for love, forgiveness, and healing. As we move forward, these lessons do not serve merely as reminders of the trials we have weathered but as luminous beacons, illuminating our path with the insights and connections we have forged along the way.

Our journey has deepened our understanding of love's many forms and its resilience. Love has shown itself to be a sanctuary in times of storm, a binding force when the fabric of our family seemed at risk of unraveling. It is the quiet moments of shared vulnerability, the collective determination to rebuild from the ashes of our past, that have revealed the true strength and depth of love. This love is not static but dynamic, growing and evolving with every challenge faced, every obstacle overcome. It is a testament to the fact that, even in the depths of grief, love can flourish, transforming pain into a deeper sense of connection and understanding.

The complexities of navigating loss have taught us the value of grace—grace towards ourselves and each other as we traverse the uneven terrain of grief. Loss has a way of laying bare the fragility of existence, prompting a profound appreciation for the fleeting moments of joy and connection. Through this journey, we have learned that to honor our losses is to allow them to shape us, not as marks of what we have lost but as part of the intricate mosaic of who we are becoming. The grace found in navigating loss lies in the acceptance of its transformative potential, allowing us to carry forward the legacies of those we've loved and lost with dignity and love.

Chapter 7: The Empty Nest Refilled

The journey through life's various stages often brings with it an expected sequence of events, one of which is the transition to an "empty nest." This period, traditionally viewed as a time when parents adjust to living without their children at home, is often associated with both the sorrow of separation and the quietude of a house no longer filled with the bustling energy of youth. However, our experience diverged significantly from this expected path, transforming what would have been a quieter life stage into a vibrant, challenging, and enriching chapter that we came to know as our "refilled nest."

The arrival of Jack and John into our lives marked the beginning of this unexpected journey. Far from the quiet emptiness we had anticipated, our home became alive with the sounds of laughter, conversation, and the occasional clatter of activity that accompanies the presence of young individuals. This transition was not merely a physical refilling of space but a profound expansion of our hearts and understanding of family. The notion of the empty nest, with its implications of loss and silence, was replaced by a sense of purpose, connection, and the warmth of a home once again teeming with life.

Embracing this refilled nest required us to adapt and grow in ways we hadn't envisioned. The routines we had settled into were reshaped to accommodate school schedules, extracurricular activities, and the emotional needs of two young souls navigating the complexities of loss and change. These adaptations were not without their challenges. Balancing the demands of this new family dynamic with our own needs and aspirations tested our patience, communication, and resilience. Yet, each hurdle crossed and each compromise reached served to strengthen the bonds between us, forging a family unit defined by mutual support, love, and the shared journey through both hardships and joys.

This period of adjustment also brought into sharp relief the contrast between the traditional concept of an empty nest and our reality. Where others might find silence, we found dialogue; where some might experience loneliness, we discovered companionship and the joy of rediscovering the world through younger eyes. The refilled nest offered us a unique perspective on the fluidity of life stages, challenging the societal expectations that dictate what each phase should look like and offering instead a testament to the adaptability and depth of the human heart.

Moreover, the journey through our refilled nest complemented our understanding of family in profound ways. It underscored the idea that family is not defined by blood or conventional milestones but by the choice to come together, to support one another, and to build a life shared in love and understanding. The experiences of love, loss, and healing that we navigated together enriched our notion of what it means to be a family, revealing that true familial bonds are forged in the fires of adversity, compassion, and shared growth.

In reflecting on our journey with Jack and John, the concept of the empty nest refilled emerges not just as a phase of life but as a symbol of transformation and renewal. It represents the unexpected paths that life can take and the beauty that can be found in embracing change with an open heart. This chapter of our lives, marked by the laughter, tears, and love that filled our once-quiet home, taught us the invaluable lesson that sometimes, the most significant growth and the deepest connections come from the most unexpected sources.

As we continue forward, the lessons learned and the love shared within our refilled nest guide us, serving as reminders of the resilience of the human spirit and the boundless capacity for joy, healing, and renewal. Our experience challenges the traditional narrative of the empty nest, offering instead a story of hope, adaptation, and the enduring power of love to redefine the contours of our lives.

The arrival of Jack and John into our lives marked a profound shift in the narrative we had anticipated for our family. As we stood at the threshold of what we believed would be a quieter chapter, our home instead burgeoned with new life, echoing with the sounds of youth and the vibrant energy of adolescence. This transition, while unexpected, unfolded as a testament to the capacity for love, adaptability, and growth at any stage of life.

Our decision to open our home and hearts to Jack and John was driven by a mixture of compassion, a sense of responsibility, and an unspoken longing for the richness that family life imbues. This choice represented a significant pivot from our envisioned future, steering us away from the calm predictability of an empty nest and into the dynamic, often unpredictable world of parenting once more.

The initial days following their arrival were a whirlwind of activity and adjustment. Our once-quiet mornings were replaced with the hustle of preparing for school, while evenings revolved around homework, dinner, and attempts to foster a sense of normalcy within our newly formed family unit. This shift demanded not just a logistical recalibration of our daily lives but a deep emotional adjustment as we sought to understand and meet the needs of two young individuals who had experienced profound loss.

The adjustments required in embracing our new family dynamic were multifaceted. For Andrew and me, it meant relearning the art of parenting—this time, to children who were not our own by birth but whom we had come to love deeply. It involved navigating the complexities of school schedules, extracurricular activities, and the myriad challenges that accompany adolescence. But beyond these practicalities, it demanded an emotional attunement to Jack and John's needs, an understanding of their grief, and a commitment to providing them with a stable, loving environment.

This transition was characterized by a series of trials and triumphs. There were moments of frustration and misunderstanding, inevitable in the process of blending lives and histories. Yet, there were also moments of profound connection and joy—breakthroughs in communication, shared laughter over dinner, and the gradual emergence of trust and affection that began to weave us together as a family.

Embracing Jack and John into our lives brought with it a richness that transcended the challenges. The joys of parenting—witnessing their achievements, supporting their dreams, and simply being part of their daily lives—offered a fulfillment that we had not anticipated. Each milestone, whether academic, personal, or otherwise, became a celebration of their resilience and our collective journey.

Moreover, this transition offered us an opportunity for personal growth. It challenged us to be more patient, understanding, and flexible, pushing us to evolve in our roles as caregivers and mentors. The responsibility of guiding Jack and John through their adolescent years, while helping them navigate their grief, became a powerful catalyst for our own development, deepening our capacity for empathy and compassion.

The arrival of Jack and John reframed our understanding of family and purpose. It underscored the notion that family is not solely defined by biological ties but by the bonds of love, support, and shared experience. Our decision to welcome them into our lives, though borne from a tragic circumstance, brought with it a renewed sense of purpose and a deeper appreciation for the complexities and beauty of family life.

As we look back on this pivotal chapter, it is clear that the arrival of Jack and John was not just an addition to our family but a transformation. It reshaped our home, our hearts, and our future in ways we could never have imagined. In embracing them, we discovered the boundless nature of love, the resilience of the human spirit, and the profound joy that comes from opening one's life to others. Our journey together, marked by the challenges and triumphs of building a new family dynamic, stands as a testament to the power of love to heal, unite, and create new paths where none seemed to exist.

The transformation of our home and lives with the arrival of Jack and John marked a profound shift in our journey as individuals and as a couple. This transition, from an anticipated quietness to a bustling household, propelled us into a phase of adaptation that tested and ultimately strengthened the very foundations of our relationship and family structure. The concept of adapting to our refilled nest encapsulates a multifaceted journey of adjustment, learning, and growth, profoundly altering our roles, responsibilities, and even the spaces that surround us.

The inclusion of Jack and John into our lives necessitated a reevaluation of our roles not just as parents but as partners. The dynamics of our relationship underwent a transformation, as we navigated the delicate balance between the needs of our new family members and the sanctity of our bond as a couple. This balancing act involved a conscious effort to maintain open lines of communication, ensuring that our own relationship remained a steadfast priority amidst the whirlwind of parenting responsibilities. We found ourselves engaging in deeper conversations, not only about logistical matters like schedules and activities but also about our emotions, fears, and hopes for this new chapter. These discussions served as the bedrock for our adapted roles, guiding us through the uncharted territory of parenting once more, while also safeguarding the intimacy and strength of our partnership.

The practical aspect of adapting to our refilled nest involved a significant shift in how we managed daily responsibilities. Tasks that were once divided became a shared endeavor, from the mundane routines of household management to the more complex challenges of addressing the emotional and developmental needs of Jack and John . This sharing of responsibilities fostered a deeper sense of teamwork and solidarity between us, as we took turns being the anchor for our family, allowing each other moments of rest and personal space. It was in these moments of shared duty and support that we rediscovered the strength of our union, a reminder that together, we were capable of overcoming any challenge.

Beyond the emotional and relational adjustments, adapting to our refilled nest also had a tangible, physical dimension. Our home, once a canvas for our individual and collective aspirations, became a living reflection of our expanded family. Bedrooms were reimagined, common spaces were revitalized, and areas once reserved for personal hobbies or future plans were transformed to accommodate the vibrant energy of two young lives. This reconfiguration of our physical space was not merely an exercise in logistics but a manifestation of our commitment to creating an environment that was welcoming, comforting, and reflective of the personalities and needs of each family member.

This transformation extended beyond the walls of individual rooms to encompass the very essence of our home. It became a space where laughter echoed, where conversations lingered well into the night, and where the traces of our individual and collective journeys intertwined to form a tapestry of family life. In redefining these spaces, we also redefined what our home represented: a sanctuary of love, understanding, and belonging for all of us.

Ultimately, the process of adapting to our refilled nest served as a powerful metaphor for the broader transformations we experienced. Just as our home evolved to reflect the needs and characters of its new occupants, so too did our identities, relationships, and perspectives. This period of adjustment highlighted the incredible capacity for growth and adaptation that lies within us, revealing that the essence of family extends far beyond the conventional boundaries of biology or expectation.

As we continue on this journey, the lessons learned and the changes embraced in adapting to our refilled nest remain a testament to the resilience, love, and unyielding support that define our family. It stands as a reminder that in the face of unexpected challenges and changes, the strength of our bond and the warmth of our home can not only endure but flourish, creating a nurturing environment where each member can grow, thrive, and find solace.

The evolution of our family, marked by the transition from an anticipated empty nest to a vibrantly refilled one, offers a rich exploration of contrasts and complements within the fabric of family life. This experience, divergent from the traditional trajectory many envision for their later years, challenges conventional narratives while also enriching our understanding of what it truly means to be a family.

Traditionally, the empty nest phase is characterized by a newfound quiet, a spaciousness that invites parents to rediscover themselves and each other in the absence of their child-rearing roles. It's often depicted as a bittersweet period of adjustment, where the silence of the home echoes the departure of grown children. In stark contrast, our home's transition was filled with the noise of life in full swing—the laughter, debates, and footsteps of Jack and John infusing our days with a dynamic energy that reshaped our daily existence.

This contrast between expectation and reality forced us to reexamine our preconceived notions about this life stage. Instead of navigating the silence, we found ourselves orchestrating the harmony of a household bustling with activity. The quiet moments we had anticipated became rare jewels, cherished amidst the lively rhythm of our refilled nest. This shift was not merely about the physical presence of Jack and John but about the emotional and psychological adaptation to our expanded family dynamic.

Yet, within this contrast lies a profound complement to our understanding of family. The refilling of our nest underscored the truth that family transcends biological ties, built instead on the foundations of love, support, and a commitment to shared growth. Jack and John, though not born to us, became ours through the bonds we forged in the crucible of shared experiences. Their arrival expanded our hearts and taught us that family is not defined by lineage but by the choices we make to connect, to care, and to hold each other up through life's journey.

This realization brought with it a unique blend of joys and challenges. Witnessing Jack and John navigate their own paths of growth, from academic achievements to personal milestones, filled us with a profound sense of pride and purpose. These moments of celebration were not just markers of their development but affirmations of our family's resilience and capacity to foster an environment where love and support fuel progress.

Conversely, the complexities of integrating Jack and John into our lives tested our resilience in unexpected ways. Their grief, a shadow of loss that followed them, demanded that we navigate our own feelings while providing them with the stability and compassion needed to heal. This aspect of our journey highlighted the boundless capacity of the human heart to love and adapt. It taught us that true strength lies in vulnerability, in the willingness to open our hearts to the pain and joy of others, and in finding joy in the most unexpected places.

The challenges we faced, from adjusting our routines to addressing the emotional upheavals that occasionally swept through our household, were significant. Yet, they were also avenues for growth, pushing us to develop a deeper empathy, to communicate more openly, and to reinforce the bonds that held us together as a family. Through every obstacle, we found moments of connection and understanding that enriched our lives in ways we could never have anticipated.

Our journey through the contrasts and complements of the refilled nest has woven a tapestry rich with love, resilience, and the joy of unexpected blessings. It has reshaped our understanding of family, revealing it to be an entity not confined by conventional definitions but defined by the depth of our connections and the strength of our commitment to one another. In embracing both the challenges and the joys of this unique life stage, we have discovered the true essence of family: a dynamic, ever-evolving structure built on the foundations of love, support, and the shared journey through the complexities of life.

As we continue forward, the lessons learned from navigating the contrasts and complements of our refilled nest remain invaluable. They serve as reminders of our capacity for love and adaptation, reinforcing the belief that family, in all its forms, is a testament to the enduring power of the human heart to find unity and joy in the most unexpected circumstances.

As we stand on the precipice of the future, the concept of our refilled nest echoes as a powerful testament to the multifaceted dimensions of love, the serendipity of life's journey, and the indomitable resilience of familial bonds. This unique chapter in our lives, far from being an endpoint, opens up new horizons of understanding and possibilities, challenging the conventional narratives associated with the transition to an empty nest. It heralds a narrative brimming with hope, renewal, and the profound realization that life's most impactful moments of connection and personal growth often stem from the least expected sources.

Our experience has fundamentally reshaped our perspective on family, on the cycles of leaving and returning that characterize the ebb and flow of life. The traditional notion of the empty nest, with its undertones of loss and solitude, has been supplanted by a vibrant tableau of life, marked by the laughter, challenges, and the warm chaos of a home once again filled with youthful energy and potential. This shift underscores the importance of maintaining flexibility in the face of life's uncertainties, of being open to change, and of the incredible value embedded in second chances—not just for those we've welcomed into our home but for ourselves as well.

The arrival of Jack and John, and the journey we've undertaken together, has imbued us with a deeper appreciation for the complex, often unpredictable tapestry of life. It has taught us that family is not just a static unit defined by biological ties or traditional milestones but a dynamic, evolving entity shaped by choices, shared experiences, and the collective will to support and uplift one another. This understanding has been a source of strength, guiding us through the challenges of adjustment and integration, and illuminating the path toward a future filled with promise and potential.

As we embrace the lessons learned from our refilled nest, we find ourselves imbued with a renewed sense of purpose and a richer appreciation for the intricate beauty of life's journey. These lessons remind us of the inherent gift that is family, in whatever form it takes—a gift that fills our home with love, challenges us to grow beyond our perceived limits, and inspires us to approach each new chapter with openness and optimism.

Looking forward, we are guided not by a blueprint of expectations but by the principles of love, resilience, and adaptability that have defined our journey thus far. We are committed to fostering an environment where every member of our family feels valued, supported, and empowered to pursue their dreams. We stand ready to face the future with open hearts, embracing the unknown with the confidence that whatever challenges or opportunities it may bring, we will navigate them together, strengthened by the bonds we've forged and the love that binds us.

In sum, our journey through the refilled nest phase has not just filled our home with renewed life but has also expanded our hearts and minds, offering a profound reminder that the essence of family lies in the shared journey of love, support, and mutual growth. It reaffirms our belief in the transformative power of love and the endless possibilities that await us as we step into the future together, armed with the lessons of the past and the hope for what lies ahead.

Nest Refilled:
A Journey of Grit, Grace, and Renewal

Chapter 8: Navigating Adolescence Anew

Starting afresh on the adventure of parenting adolescents, especially Jack and John, amid their tapestry of grief and the distinct trajectory our family has followed, brought forth a myriad of intricate challenges and chances for growth. Adolescence, already a turbulent phase in ideal conditions, became even more intricate with the added layers of mourning and adaptation that both boys carried. This stage of our journey demanded a careful equilibrium of mentorship, encouragement, and empathy as we traversed the unfamiliar terrain of nurturing teenagers amidst an unconventional family backdrop.

Undertaking the task of parenting adolescents, particularly given the distinctive circumstances surrounding Jack and John, necessitated a thorough exploration of their perspective. Their teenage years weren't solely a time of physical and emotional development but were deeply intertwined with the profound loss they had faced. Losing both parents during such a crucial, formative period placed them in a realm of grief that profoundly influenced their adolescent journey. It became essential for us to acknowledge that their actions, sometimes perceived as typical teenage defiance, were intricately layered with complexities stemming from their bereavement.

To truly understand their world, we had to become students of their behaviors, emotions, and the unspoken grief that often lingered in the air. Withdrawal, for instance, wasn't merely a desire for independence but sometimes a retreat into themselves, where the pain felt more manageable. Anger wasn't always a reaction to boundaries or rules but could be an expression of the deep-seated injustice they felt at having their parents taken from them. Confusion often stemmed from trying to navigate the normal challenges of adolescence while also processing their profound loss.

This realization shifted our approach significantly. We began to see the importance of creating an environment where Jack and John felt seen and heard, where their feelings were validated, and where they could express their grief without fear of judgment. It involved active listening, where we not just heard their words but sought to understand the emotions and experiences behind them. We encouraged open conversations about their parents, their memories, and their feelings of loss, making it clear that their parents' absence was a loss for our family as a whole, not just a personal tragedy for them.

Moreover, understanding their world meant recognizing the fluctuating nature of grief in adolescence. Grief could be a chameleon, changing colors with the seasons of their lives. It required us to be flexible and responsive, to recognize the signs of emerging sadness or frustration, and to offer support without forcing conversations or emotions they were not ready to engage with. This approach helped in making our home a safe haven for them, a place where the complexities of their feelings could coexist with the everyday challenges of growing up.

In our efforts to understand their world, we also sought external support when necessary, including counselors who specialized in adolescent grief. This provided Jack and John with additional perspectives and coping mechanisms, reinforcing the message that they were not alone in their journey. It also offered us insights into how best to support them, equipping us with the tools to navigate the intricate dance of providing guidance while respecting their need for autonomy.

Through this journey of understanding, we learned that adolescence, particularly for children who have experienced significant loss, is a tapestry woven with threads of resilience, vulnerability, and the ongoing search for identity. Recognizing the impact of Jack and John's losses meant acknowledging that their path through adolescence would be uniquely challenging. Yet, it also opened up opportunities for growth, healing, and the deepening of our familial bonds. By striving to see the world through their eyes, we not only fostered a deeper connection with them but also enriched our collective experience as a family, navigating the complexities of loss and adolescence with empathy, love, and an unwavering commitment to understanding their world.

Creating a safe space for Jack and John became a fundamental goal as we navigated the complexities of our refilled nest, understanding that the emotional terrain they were traversing required a haven where they could openly express themselves without fear of judgment or dismissal. This endeavor went beyond the physical safety of our home; it extended into the emotional and psychological realms, where true expression and healing could take place.

Fostering open lines of communication was our initial step toward building this sanctuary. This effort was about more than just encouraging dialogue; it was about cultivating an atmosphere where vulnerability was met with empathy, and silence could speak as loudly as words. We dedicated time each day to simply be together, whether during meals or in the quiet moments before bedtime, signaling that our availability to listen was constant and unwavering. These moments became the cornerstone of our communication, a daily testament to our commitment to their well-being.

In these exchanges, we emphasized the validity and importance of their feelings, irrespective of their nature.

Whether they were grappling with grief, wrestling with adolescent anxieties, or celebrating small victories, we wanted Jack and John to know that their emotions were seen and valued. This validation was crucial in cultivating their trust, gradually opening doors to deeper conversations about their fears, hopes, and memories of their parents.

Moreover, recognizing that communication comes in various forms, we encouraged them to explore alternative outlets for expression. Art became a powerful medium for Jack, a canvas where colors and shapes could articulate the emotions for which he had no words. John found solace and expression in music, where rhythms and melodies offered him a language to communicate his inner world. These outlets were not just about self-expression but were integral to their healing process, providing them with tools to navigate their emotions and share their inner experiences with us in non-verbal ways.

The establishment of our home as a sanctuary of unconditional acceptance was a deliberate process, marked by our consistent efforts to demonstrate love and support. This meant actively challenging societal norms that stigmatize vulnerability, especially in young men, and dismantling any notion that strength is synonymous with silence. By modeling emotional openness ourselves, sharing our feelings, uncertainties, and even our struggles with grief, we aimed to show Jack and John that true strength lies in the courage to be vulnerable.

Creating this safe space also meant being proactive in addressing any signs of distress and reassuring them that seeking help, whether from family members or professionals, was a sign of courage and self-awareness, not weakness. This approach fostered an environment where emotional health was prioritized, and support was readily available, ensuring they never felt alone in their journey.

Nest Refilled:
A Journey of Grit, Grace, and Renewal

As we reflect on the significance of creating a safe space, it becomes clear that this environment was not just beneficial for Jack and John but transformative for our family. It reinforced our home as a foundation of trust, openness, and healing, where each member could grow, explore, and express themselves freely. This sanctuary of unconditional acceptance became the bedrock upon which we built our family's resilience, navigating the challenges and joys of adolescence with the assurance that, within our home, every emotion had a place, and every voice was heard and cherished.

Supporting Jack and John through their individual paths of adolescence and healing required a nuanced understanding of their personalities, grief processes, and coping mechanisms. It became clear early on that a one-size-fits-all approach would not suffice; instead, we endeavored to meet them where they were, offering tailored support that respected their individuality.

For Jack, introspection was his refuge. He was more inclined to internalize his emotions, finding it challenging to articulate his feelings through words. Recognizing this, we sought activities that allowed him to engage with his inner world in a more comfortable, non-verbal manner. Reading became a significant outlet for him, offering both an escape and a mirror to his own experiences through the stories of others. Literature provided Jack with diverse perspectives on loss, resilience, and the complexities of human emotions, facilitating a silent dialogue with his own grief.

Music, too, played a pivotal role in Jack's journey. Whether playing instruments or losing himself in the melodies of his favorite songs, music offered him a language beyond words, a means to express and process his emotions in a deeply personal and cathartic way. This engagement with music not only served as a therapeutic outlet but also as a bridge, connecting his internal experiences with the external world in a manner that felt safe and authentic to him.

John, on the other hand, manifested his grief and sought healing through connection and physical activity. He was naturally more expressive and found solace in shared experiences and the camaraderie of team sports. Encouraging his involvement in sports and group activities provided him with a constructive outlet for his energy and emotions. These activities fostered a sense of belonging and achievement, offering John a platform to build confidence, form friendships, and engage with a supportive community outside the home. The structure and discipline of sports, coupled with the unconditional support of his teammates and coaches, became integral to his process of healing and growth.

Our individualized approach to supporting Jack and John underscored our commitment to their unique needs and paths. By offering them the space to explore and engage with activities that resonated with their personal ways of coping, we affirmed their right to grieve and heal in ways that felt natural to them. This respect for their individuality not only facilitated their healing but also fostered a deeper sense of trust and understanding within our family dynamics.

In embracing their distinct journeys, we learned the importance of flexibility, patience, and the power of simply being present. Supporting their individual paths became a journey of its own—a journey marked by learning, adaptation, and the profound realization that healing, in all its forms, is a testament to the resilience of the human spirit and the transformative power of love and understanding.

In the journey of redefining our family dynamics and guiding Jack and John through their adolescence, fostering resilience and independence emerged as a pivotal theme. Understanding that the landscape of their young lives had been irrevocably altered by loss, we recognized the necessity of equipping them with the skills to navigate future challenges with strength and self-assurance. This endeavor was not about shielding them from the hardships of life but about empowering them to face these challenges head-on, with a toolbox of strategies and a foundation of confidence.

Central to fostering their resilience was the cultivation of problem-solving skills. We encouraged Jack and John to approach obstacles not as insurmountable barriers but as puzzles to be solved. This process involved guiding them through the steps of identifying the problem, brainstorming potential solutions, evaluating these options, and then implementing and reflecting on the outcomes. Through real-life applications, from academic challenges to interpersonal conflicts, they learned the value of critical thinking and adaptability. These experiences taught them that setbacks could be learning opportunities, laying the groundwork for resilience in the face of future adversities.

Equally important was the development of self-awareness and emotional intelligence. We fostered environments where open discussions about feelings, motivations, and reactions were normalized. Jack and John were encouraged to reflect on their emotions, to recognize their triggers, and to understand the impact of their actions on themselves and others. This self-exploration was supported through activities like journaling, meditation, and, when necessary, therapeutic intervention, which provided them with the space and tools to delve into their inner landscapes. Developing emotional intelligence not only bolstered their resilience but also enhanced their capacity for empathy, improving their interactions and relationships with others.

Perseverance was another cornerstone of our approach. We shared stories of personal and historical figures who overcame obstacles through persistence, highlighting the idea that success often comes after numerous attempts and failures. Celebrating their efforts and growth in all endeavors, whether successfully mastering a new skill or navigating a particularly challenging day, reinforced the concept that progress and resilience are often the results of perseverance. These celebrations served to boost their self-esteem and underscored the intrinsic value of their efforts, irrespective of the outcome.

Fostering independence was about providing Jack and John with a sense of agency over their lives. We encouraged them to make decisions, from daily choices about their activities and interests to larger decisions about their future paths. This empowerment was balanced with guidance, ensuring they had the support needed while also granting them the freedom to explore their identities and make their own mistakes. This balance of autonomy and support nurtured their sense of independence, preparing them to navigate the complexities of life with confidence.

Through these strategies, we aimed to equip Jack and John with the resilience and independence necessary to thrive. This process was iterative, filled with moments of triumph and challenge, each contributing to their development. By emphasizing problem-solving, self-awareness, perseverance, and agency, we sought to instill in them not just the skills to face life's challenges but the belief in their own capacity to overcome them. This journey of fostering resilience and independence was as much about preparing them for the future as it was about honoring their present experiences, acknowledging their strength, and celebrating their growth every step of the way.

In the nuanced journey of parenting Jack and John through their adolescent years, particularly against the backdrop of their earlier losses, one of the most intricate paths we navigated was finding the equilibrium between guidance and autonomy. This delicate balance—acting as a compass to provide direction while simultaneously allowing them the freedom to explore their own decisions—was pivotal in fostering their growth into resilient and independent individuals.

Embarking on this dance required us to carefully calibrate our approach, ensuring that our guidance empowered rather than overshadowed their journey to self-discovery. It was about more than just setting boundaries and expectations; it was about instilling in them the confidence to trust their instincts and the wisdom to recognize their own strengths and limitations. This process involved an ongoing dialogue, one where their voices and perspectives were given weight, allowing them to actively participate in the decision-making processes that affected their lives.

Providing guidance while respecting their autonomy meant offering advice and insights with an open hand, allowing Jack and John the space to accept or reject our suggestions based on their own judgments. This approach was rooted in the understanding that the ultimate goal was not to mold them into versions of who we thought they should be but to support them in becoming their most authentic selves. It involved sharing our experiences and the lessons we've learned, not as directives but as maps they could consult on their own journeys.

Allowing them the autonomy to make their own decisions also meant embracing the inevitability of mistakes and missteps. We recognized that some of life's most enduring lessons are learned not through caution but through the consequences of our choices. This acknowledgment did not lessen our instinct to protect them from potential harm, but it underscored the importance of allowing them to navigate their own challenges, providing support and guidance from the sidelines rather than steering their course directly.

Navigating the waters of guidance and autonomy required us to be adaptable, to recognize when to step in with a steadying hand and when to step back and allow them to lead. This adaptability was crucial as Jack and John each navigated their own unique paths through adolescence, presenting different needs and challenges that required us to continually reassess our approach. As they grew and evolved, so too did our understanding of how best to support them, ensuring that our guidance was both relevant and respectful of their burgeoning independence.

At the heart of this delicate balance was the fostering of trust and confidence—trust in their ability to make sound decisions and confidence in our unwavering support, regardless of the outcomes. This foundation of trust and confidence was essential not just for their sense of security but for the deepening of our familial bonds. It reinforced the notion that while we were there to provide guidance and support, we also respected their autonomy and their capacity to learn, grow, and make decisions for themselves.

In navigating the intricate dance between guidance and autonomy, we endeavored to provide Jack and John with the tools, wisdom, and freedom they needed to chart their own courses. This journey, marked by constant learning and adjustment, highlighted the profound capacity for growth and understanding that emerges when we strike the right balance—empowering them to navigate the complexities of adolescence and beyond with resilience, confidence, and a sense of ownership over their destinies.

In navigating the multifaceted journey of adolescence with Jack and John, particularly in light of their profound losses, we quickly recognized that the support within the four walls of our home, though substantial and rooted in love, might not encompass the entirety of their needs. Adolescence is a complex period of emotional, psychological, and social development, made even more intricate by the grief and adjustments they were facing. To address this, we sought to extend our support network beyond our immediate family, leveraging external resources that could provide additional perspectives and strategies for coping and healing. This decision was rooted in the understanding that a diverse support system could offer a more holistic approach to their well-being.

One of the first steps we took was to engage with professional counseling services. Recognizing the stigma often associated with mental health support, we approached this with sensitivity and openness, emphasizing the strength and courage it takes to seek help. For Jack and John, counseling offered a safe, neutral space where they could explore their feelings with someone outside the family dynamic. This external perspective was invaluable, not just for them but for us as well, as it provided insights into their inner worlds that they might not have been comfortable sharing directly with us. Counseling became a cornerstone of their healing process, equipping them with coping strategies tailored to their individual experiences and personalities, and facilitating a deeper understanding of their grief and how it intersected with the normal challenges of adolescence.

In addition to individual counseling, we explored the benefits of support groups. These groups provided a communal space where Jack and John could connect with peers who had similar experiences of loss. This sense of community was instrumental in normalizing their feelings, allowing them to see that they were not alone in their journey. The shared stories and experiences within these groups fostered a sense of belonging and understanding that was difficult to replicate in other settings. For Jack and John, these groups were a testament to the power of shared experiences in healing, offering them different perspectives on coping and resilience, and reminding them that their feelings were valid and shared by others.

Leveraging these external supports enriched the boys' overall support system in ways that extended far beyond what we could provide alone. It introduced them to a broader network of resources, perspectives, and coping mechanisms that complemented the love and support they received at home. This holistic approach to their well-being not only aided in their healing and development but also reinforced our family's resilience, providing us with additional tools and knowledge to navigate the challenges of adolescence and loss together.

Engaging with counseling and support groups underscored our commitment to Jack and John's well-being, illustrating the importance of a multi-faceted support system in addressing the complex needs of adolescents navigating grief. It highlighted the value of external perspectives and the role of community in the healing process, reminding us that while the journey through adolescence and grief can be profoundly challenging, it does not have to be walked alone. Through leveraging these external supports, we were able to provide Jack and John with a richer, more comprehensive network of care, one that honored their individual experiences while fostering a path toward healing and growth within the embrace of our family.

Navigating the waters of adolescence anew with Jack and John has been a profound exploration into the realms of growth, transformation, and the unyielding strength of familial bonds. This journey, intricately laced with the challenges of navigating grief and building new relationships, has unfolded a rich tapestry of experiences, illuminating the resilience and capacity for love that defines our family.

Nest Refilled:
A Journey of Grit, Grace, and Renewal

As we ventured into this chapter, the uncertainty of blending our lives with Jack and John's presented itself as a formidable challenge. Yet, it was within this uncertainty that we found unexpected opportunities for joy and profound learning. Adolescence, a critical phase of individual development, became a shared journey of discovery for us all. We witnessed Jack and John's transformation from boys navigating their grief to young men forging their identities with resilience and compassion. Their evolution was not just a testament to their inner strength but also to the power of the supportive environment we cultivated together.

This unique chapter of adolescence, juxtaposed against the backdrop of loss and the unconventional path our family has taken, offered insights into the elasticity of the human spirit. Jack and John, each armed with their own dreams, passions, and perspectives, navigated the complexities of their experiences, transforming challenges into opportunities for growth. Their ability to adapt, to find joy in moments big and small, and to extend empathy to others has been a source of inspiration.

The bonds of love and understanding that have flourished between us served as the bedrock of our journey. Through every triumph and setback, the foundation of our family has been strengthened, highlighting the indispensable role of shared experiences in forging deep connections. It's these connections that have illuminated our path forward, guiding us through moments of doubt and reaffirming the significance of our united journey.

As we reflect on the path traversed thus far, it's clear that the journey through adolescence with Jack and John has been a catalyst for growth—not just for them but for us as well. It challenged our preconceived notions of family, parenting, and resilience, offering a richer, more nuanced understanding of these concepts. This experience has underscored the transformative impact of love, patience, and understanding in navigating the complex waters of adolescent development.

The insights and lessons gleaned from this chapter have become integral threads in the fabric of our family's narrative, enriching our collective story with layers of hope, wisdom, and a deeper appreciation for the nuances of adolescence. It serves as a poignant reminder of the opportunities for connection, growth, and reaffirmation of our commitments to each other that lie within the complexities of raising teenagers.

As we continue to move forward, the journey with Jack and John reinforces our belief in the enduring strength of family bonds and the transformative power of love and understanding. It's a testament to the idea that, even against the backdrop of loss and change, families can thrive, grounded in mutual support and a shared commitment to navigating life's challenges together.

Embracing this journey has not only facilitated the emergence of two remarkable young men but has also catalyzed our own development as individuals and as a unit. The evolution of our family dynamics, enriched by the challenges and triumphs of navigating adolescence anew, stands as a beacon of hope and resilience. It affirms that within the complexities of teenage years lies the potential for profound growth and connection, reminding us of the beauty and strength inherent in the shared journey of life. This chapter, a significant milestone in our collective journey, leaves us with a sense of gratitude for the lessons learned, the challenges overcome, and the unbreakable bonds forged along the way.

Nest Refilled:
A Journey of Grit, Grace, and Renewal

Chapter 9: Towards Independence and Identity

As Jack and John edge closer to the precipice of adulthood, our family finds itself navigating the nuanced transition from adolescence to independence. This phase, marked by their quest for self-identity and the decisions shaping their futures, unfolds against the backdrop of our support, guidance, and the gradual rediscovery of our own identities beyond the confines of parental roles.

Fostering autonomy in Jack and John has been a nuanced process, deeply intertwined with our desire to see them grow into self-reliant, confident individuals. As they navigate the precipice of adulthood, their journey is marked not only by the tangible milestones commonly associated with growing up but also by the intangible process of self-discovery. This exploration of their identities—shaped by their unique passions, beliefs, and aspirations—has become a central theme in our approach to parenting during these transformative years.

Creating an environment that encourages autonomy involves a deliberate stepping back, a practice that goes against the instinctual pull of traditional parenting. It requires trust and faith in their abilities to make decisions, coupled with the understanding that mistakes are not just inevitable but essential for growth. We have strived to make our home a place where independence is not just allowed but encouraged, where Jack and John feel free to express their opinions, explore their interests, and make choices that reflect their personal values.

This autonomy extends to all areas of their lives, from the academic choices they make—encouraging them to pursue subjects and activities that genuinely interest them, rather than those we might prefer—to decisions about their social lives and personal relationships. Our role has shifted from directive to supportive, offering guidance when asked and refraining from intervening unless necessary. This respect for their ability to navigate their own lives is a cornerstone of fostering their autonomy.

Equally important to granting autonomy is ensuring that a safety net of support is ever-present. This safety net is not just about being there to catch them when they fall but about providing a foundation of unconditional love and support that empowers them to take risks. It involves active listening, offering advice when it's sought, and always reinforcing the message that their worth is not contingent on their successes or failures. This balanced approach helps mitigate the fear of failure, encouraging them to view challenges as opportunities to learn and grow.

Navigating the balance between fostering autonomy and providing support and guidance has been one of our greatest challenges and rewards. It has required constant adjustment and communication, ensuring that our support neither stifles their independence nor leaves them feeling unsupported. This delicate dance is a testament to our commitment to their growth as autonomous individuals, equipped with the confidence, resilience, and self-awareness to face life's challenges.

As we continue to support Jack and John in their journey towards independence, we do so with the knowledge that fostering autonomy is a dynamic process, one that evolves as they do. It's a process that not only prepares them for the challenges of adulthood but also strengthens our bond as a family, grounded in mutual respect, understanding, and an unwavering commitment to their individual paths of growth and discovery.

Nest Refilled:
A Journey of Grit, Grace, and Renewal

Supporting Jack and John as they make decisions about their futures is a practice rooted deeply in respect for their autonomy and a commitment to fostering their self-confidence. This phase of their lives is punctuated with significant decisions—from choosing academic paths and career aspirations to navigating personal relationships. Our role in this transformative period has evolved; we are no longer the directors of their lives but rather consultants, offering guidance and insights when solicited, and standing back to allow them the space to chart their own courses.

This evolution in our role is indicative of our respect for their maturity and burgeoning independence. We strive to be a sounding board for their ideas and decisions, offering perspectives based on our experiences while being mindful not to impose our own wishes or expectations upon them. This approach underscores the value we place on their ability to make informed choices, acknowledging that the journey to adulthood is marked by learning to navigate the complexities of life's decisions.

Central to supporting their decision-making process is the reinforcement of their confidence. We aim to instill in Jack and John a sense of self-belief that emboldens them to take ownership of their choices. This involves a delicate balance of encouraging exploration and risk-taking while also being present to guide and advise when they seek it. Celebrating their successes, no matter how small, serves to bolster their confidence, reminding them of their capabilities and resilience. Similarly, providing a supportive presence during setbacks or challenges is crucial. These moments are opportunities for learning and growth, and our response to their difficulties can either reinforce their self-efficacy or undermine it. We emphasize that setbacks are not failures but part of the learning process, offering comfort and perspective to help them navigate these experiences.

Acknowledging that successes and setbacks are both integral to their growth journey is a fundamental aspect of our support. Successes are moments of affirmation, milestones that mark their progress and achievements. We celebrate these with genuine enthusiasm, recognizing their hard work and dedication. Conversely, setbacks are treated with equal importance, not as moments of defeat but as opportunities for reflection and development. We encourage Jack and John to analyze these experiences, to understand what can be learned from them, and to recognize that setbacks are not indicative of their worth or potential.

Supporting Jack and John's decision-making processes is an ongoing journey, one that requires patience, understanding, and a deep commitment to their individual paths to adulthood. By acting as consultants rather than directors, we respect their autonomy and foster their ability to navigate life's decisions confidently. Whether through successes or setbacks, our support is unwavering, rooted in the belief that these experiences are invaluable components of their growth. This approach not only aids in their development into self-assured, independent individuals but also strengthens the bonds of trust and communication within our family, ensuring that, no matter the decisions they face, they know they are supported, valued, and loved.

As Jack and John navigate the path towards independence, their journey inadvertently mirrors our own—a parallel transition where Andrew and I find ourselves at a crossroads, confronting and rediscovering our identities beyond the realms of parental roles. This phase, characterized by introspection and exploration, has unfurled as an opportunity not merely to fill the void created by their growing autonomy but to celebrate our evolution both as individuals and as a couple.

The gradual shift towards a quieter house, with Jack and John carving out their niches in the world, has opened up spaces and silences that beckon for reoccupation. This period has propelled us to delve into the layers of our own identities, peeling back the roles we've adorned for years to uncover the aspirations, interests, and passions that lay dormant or unexplored. It's a rediscovery that challenges the notion of identity as a fixed star; instead, we find it to be a constellation, ever-expanding and illuminated by new experiences and insights.

For Andrew, this journey has meant revisiting old hobbies and passions that were put on pause, allowing him to weave these threads back into the fabric of his daily life. It has also opened up avenues for new interests that resonate with the person he has become over the years. For me, the transition has been an exploration of newfound passions and the rekindling of old ones, alongside a deeper engagement with personal and professional aspirations that were once sidelined.

This period of self-discovery has also been pivotal in redefining our relationship. As we navigate this new phase, we find ourselves rediscovering each other, not just as parents but as individuals with evolving dreams, desires, and dimensions. This rediscovery has fostered a deeper connection between us, igniting conversations that traverse beyond the domain of parenting into the realms of personal growth, aspirations, and mutual support for our individual pursuits.

The freedom to explore these new avenues has brought with it a revitalization of our partnership, reminding us of the joy in shared exploration and the strength derived from supporting each other's journeys. It's a dynamic that underscores the importance of growing together, even as we grow individually, ensuring that our relationship continues to thrive amidst the changes.

The independence of Jack and John has accorded us the freedom to embark on new adventures, be they travel, education, or creative endeavors that were once deemed impractical. This phase has encouraged us to step out of our comfort zones, to embrace the uncertainty and excitement of trying new things, and to invest in our personal and collective growth.

This exploration is not a bid to reclaim a lost youth or to fill the quiet with noise but a genuine pursuit of fulfillment and joy in the activities and passions that resonate with us now. It's an acknowledgment that growth and discovery are not confined to the early chapters of our lives but are continual processes that enrich our existence.

As we reflect on this journey of rediscovery, what becomes evident is that the transition towards independence—for Jack and John, and for us—is not just a series of logistical shifts but a profound transformation that touches the core of our identities. It's a period that challenges the static perceptions of self and relationship, inviting us to embrace the fluidity and expansiveness of our identities.

This evolution, marked by the exploration of new interests and the deepening of our relationship, is a testament to the capacity for change and growth at any stage of life. It reaffirms the idea that our identities are multifaceted and dynamic, capable of embracing new dimensions while honoring the core values and experiences that have shaped us.

As we continue to navigate this landscape of rediscovery and growth, the insights and experiences gleaned from this chapter enrich our narrative, offering a blueprint for navigating life's transitions with openness, curiosity, and a commitment to continual evolution. It underscores the beauty of embracing each chapter of life not just as a continuation but as an opportunity for renewal and discovery, celebrating the journey towards independence and identity as a family and as individuals, each with our unique paths to explore and cherish.

The journey towards independence and identity has been a significant catalyst for transformation within our family dynamics. This pivotal period, marked by Jack and John's transition into adulthood, has not only reshaped their individual paths but has also profoundly impacted the fabric of our familial relationships. As they navigate the complexities of forging their identities and making autonomous decisions, we, too, find ourselves adapting, discovering new dimensions in our connections with them, and, in the process, witnessing the evolution of our family dynamics into a more nuanced and enriched tapestry.

As Jack and John venture further into the realms of independence, their burgeoning personalities, interests, and worldviews come into sharper focus. This process of self-discovery has provided us with invaluable opportunities to engage with them on new levels, transcending the conventional roles of parent and child. We find ourselves not just as guardians but as active participants in a shared journey of growth. Conversations have deepened, reflecting a broader spectrum of topics that include their aspirations, ethical dilemmas, and perspectives on global issues. These dialogues, rich with their insights and burgeoning worldviews, offer windows into their evolving identities, revealing depths and facets that were previously unseen.

One of the most profound shifts in our family dynamics has been the emergence of a deep, mutual respect that blurs the traditional boundaries between parent and child. This respect is rooted in the acknowledgment of their autonomy and the validation of their choices and opinions. It signifies a departure from a directive approach to one that values collaboration and consultation. This newfound respect fosters an environment where each family member feels valued and heard, strengthening the bonds that tie us together and laying a solid foundation for enduring relationships as Jack and John step fully into adulthood.

The evolution of our family dynamics is also characterized by our collective navigation through the changes this transition entails. As Jack and John assert their independence, we explore what it means to be a family when the day-to-day dependencies diminish. This exploration has led us to find new ways of being together, whether through shared interests, family traditions that adapt to our changing lives, or simply finding joy in the moments we spend together. These adaptations ensure that our connection remains vibrant and meaningful, even as the nature of our interactions evolves.

Perhaps the most significant aspect of this evolving dynamic is the foundation it lays for our future relationships. By fostering an environment of openness, respect, and mutual support, we are building the groundwork for enduring bonds that will sustain us through the various chapters of life. This foundation is crucial, not just for maintaining our connection as a family but for ensuring that Jack and John feel secure in the knowledge that, regardless of where their journeys take them, they have a steadfast support system in us.

Embracing the evolution of our family dynamics requires an openness to change and an acknowledgment that growth often comes with its own set of challenges. It demands flexibility, patience, and an unwavering commitment to nurturing our relationships through the ebbs and flows of life. This period of transition has taught us that family dynamics are not static but are continually shaped by the individual journeys of its members. It has highlighted the beauty of growth, the strength derived from mutual respect, and the enduring nature of familial bonds.

As we look forward, we do so with a sense of optimism and gratitude for the journey that has brought us to this point. The evolution of our family dynamics, while at times challenging, has been an enriching experience, deepening our connections with Jack and John and with each other. It stands as a testament to the transformative power of love, understanding, and shared experiences, reminding us that, in the face of change, our family remains our most significant source of strength and support.

Embracing the journey towards independence and identity, for both Jack and John and for ourselves, has been an enlightening and transformative experience. This chapter in our family's narrative, characterized by its profound capacity for growth and deeper connections, has allowed us to witness firsthand the remarkable resilience and strength that lie at the heart of our family bonds. It's a journey marked by the dual processes of individual discovery and collective evolution, illustrating the intricate dance between nurturing autonomy and maintaining the closeness that defines us as a family.

As Jack and John venture into the realms of independence, forging their paths and exploring their identities, we've been privileged to support and witness their metamorphosis. This support, however, extends beyond mere guidance; it's a celebration of their individuality, an acknowledgment of their unique journeys, and a testament to our belief in their potential. The anticipation, hope, and occasional bittersweet pangs of letting go have underscored the complexity of this transition, revealing the multifaceted nature of parental love—a love that empowers, respects, and ultimately, lets go.

The inevitable moments of letting go, while challenging, have also brought with them a sense of pride and accomplishment. Seeing Jack and John make decisions, face challenges, and embrace their passions with confidence and resilience has been a deeply rewarding aspect of this journey. These moments not only signify their growth but also highlight the enduring strength of the foundation we've built together as a family—a foundation rooted in unconditional support, understanding, and mutual respect.

Our journey has also prompted a reflection on our roles as parents and partners, urging us to rediscover and redefine our identities beyond the confines of parenthood. This rediscovery has been an invigorating process, allowing us to pursue personal aspirations, explore new interests, and invest in our relationship. It's a parallel path of growth that mirrors the independence journey of Jack and John, reinforcing the idea that personal development is a lifelong process.

Looking towards the future, our hearts swell with optimism and excitement for what lies ahead. We envision a horizon filled with endless possibilities for Jack and John, a future where they continue to grow, thrive, and make their mark on the world. This optimism is coupled with a deep sense of gratitude for the journey thus far, for the lessons learned, the challenges overcome, and the love that has deepened with each passing day.

This phase of our family's story, rich in adaptation, learning, and an abundance of love, serves as a powerful reminder of the significance of family support in navigating the complex waters of independence and identity. It underscores our unwavering commitment to creating a family environment that champions exploration, growth, and the pursuit of personal fulfillment. It reaffirms the invaluable role of familial bonds in providing a secure foundation from which each member can confidently embark on their individual journeys.

As we embrace the ongoing journey, we do so with the knowledge that our family is bound not just by blood but by the shared experiences, challenges, and triumphs that have shaped our collective narrative. This journey, with its blend of individual and collective milestones, is a celebration of the dynamic, ever-evolving nature of family life. It is a testament to the transformative power of love, understanding, and support, highlighting the beauty of walking this path together.

As I consider our journey, I am reminded of the profound connections and growth that arise from navigating life's transitions as a family. It is a journey that illustrates the balance between supporting autonomy and fostering closeness, between celebrating individual paths and cherishing the shared journey that unites us. As we continue to navigate the evolving landscape of our lives, the experiences and insights gained from this chapter enrich our family's narrative, offering hope, wisdom, and a deeper appreciation for the journey of independence and identity—a journey we embark on together, strengthened by the bonds of love and the shared commitment to supporting one another's dreams and aspirations.

Nest Refilled:
A Journey of Grit, Grace, and Renewal

Chapter 10: Reflections on a Journey Unplanned

As we stand at the threshold of reflection, poised to look back on a journey that unfolded in the most unexpected of ways, it becomes clear that our path has been nothing short of transformative. This journey, born from a confluence of tragedy and love, has reshaped the contours of our lives, redefining our understanding of family, resilience, and the boundless capacity for growth. The story that follows is not just a recounting of events but a deep dive into the heart of what it means to come together under the shadow of loss and emerge, together, into the light of newfound understanding and connection.

When we first embarked on this path, stepping into the roles of guardians for Jack and John in the wake of unspeakable loss, we could scarcely imagine the challenges and joys that lay ahead. The sudden responsibility thrust upon us, the weight of grief, and the daunting task of forging a new family unit seemed insurmountable. Yet, as the days turned into months, and months into years, what emerged was a narrative rich with lessons learned, obstacles overcome, and moments of unexpected joy.

This introduction sets the stage for a reflective journey through the trials and triumphs that have marked our path. It is a journey characterized by the grit needed to face each new challenge, the grace to navigate the complexities of healing and understanding, and the profound growth experienced by each of us. As we recount the steps we've taken, the moments of despair and the peaks of joy, we invite you to journey with us through the chapters of our story—a story that, while marked by the pain of loss, is ultimately defined by the power of love, the resilience of the human spirit, and the unanticipated beauty of a life reshaped by circumstance.

Through this reflection, we aim not just to share our story but to illuminate the universal truths that bind us all—the strength found in vulnerability, the transformative power of compassion, and the enduring hope that guides us forward.

The early days following our sudden expansion into a family of four were marked by a palpable sense of shock and disorientation. Thrust into roles we had never anticipated, the ground Beneath us felt unsteady, charged with the raw emotion of grief and the daunting reality of our new responsibilities. Jack and John, reeling from the loss of their father, brought into our home not just their belongings but a tangible cloud of sorrow that settled into every corner, every silent moment of our newfound family life.

Adjusting to these new roles was akin to navigating a maze without a map. Overnight, our quiet routines were upended, replaced by the urgent needs of two boys grappling with an unfathomable loss. Meals, once simple affairs, became intricate dances of coaxing and comforting. Bedtimes were prolonged by whispered conversations, attempts to soothe the day's anxieties and fears. Our roles as guardians demanded more than just providing; it required us to become confidants, protectors, and the bearers of stability in a world that had shifted Beneath Jack and John's feet.

The immediate impact on our family dynamics was profound. The balance we had once taken for granted was now a thing of the past, replaced by a constant effort to forge connections, to understand and to be understood. The quiet moments we cherished became charged with the effort to communicate, to breach the walls of grief that each of us, in our way, had built around our hearts.

Those early days were a test of our resilience, a period marked by trial and error as we learned to navigate the complexities of our new reality. Yet, amidst the challenges, there were glimmers of hope—small victories in our daily battles for normalcy and moments of unexpected laughter that pierced the fog of sorrow. It was a time of profound learning and adjustment, laying the foundation for the journey of healing and growth that lay ahead. In those challenging times, the seeds of our future unity were sown, watered by tears and tended with tentative, but growing, love.

Navigating the intricate path of our unexpected family journey, we encountered numerous trials that tested our strength, patience, and resolve. Among these, the challenge of melding disparate lives into a cohesive unit stood paramount. Jack and John, each ensnared in their private labyrinths of grief, often found themselves at odds with the new family dynamics, their pain manifesting in withdrawal or bursts of frustration. For us, adapting to the sudden expansion of our family meant learning to balance the fine line between providing structure and allowing space for healing.

One significant trial was the quest for a shared language of love and understanding. Early attempts at communication often felt like speaking across vast chasms, with misinterpretations and misunderstandings further complicating our journey. However, it was through these very challenges that our most significant breakthroughs emerged. A pivotal moment came one evening, when a spontaneous family game night turned into an unexpected opening of hearts. Laughter replaced tears, and shared stories bridged the gaps between us, illuminating our common ground and fostering a sense of belonging.

Another triumph was witnessing Jack and John's gradual return to the world of the living. The first time Jack volunteered to help with dinner, a task he undertook with surprising eagerness, marked a turning point in his journey of healing. Similarly, John's first genuine laugh, unrestrained and joyful, resonated as a triumph over the shadows of sorrow that had lingered in our home. These moments, small yet profound, signaled the blossoming of trust and the deepening of our familial bonds.

Celebrating these triumphs became a crucial element of our journey, serving not only as milestones of our progress but as reminders of our collective resilience. Each breakthrough, each step forward, was a testament to the transformative power of love and patience. Through trials and triumphs alike, we carved a path forward, a narrative not just of survival but of flourishing in the face of the unexpected. Our journey, marked by both challenges and victories, reflects the indomitable spirit of a family united not by circumstance, but by an unbreakable bond of love and mutual respect.

The tapestry of our family's journey is rich with the threads of growth and transformation, each strand representing the personal and collective evolution we have undergone. In the crucible of our shared experiences, both challenging and rewarding, each of us has emerged markedly changed, stronger, and more deeply connected.

Jack, once shrouded in the silent armor of grief, has blossomed into a young man of depth and sensitivity. His journey through the tumultuous waters of loss and adaptation has revealed a resilience and empathy that astonish and inspire us. The transformation is evident in his thoughtful gaze, in his willingness to reach out, and in the maturity with which he navigates his relationships and responsibilities. His growth has been a beacon of hope, a testament to the healing power of time, understanding, and unconditional support.

John's journey has been equally profound. From the storm of emotions that once seemed to engulf him, he has found his footing, channeling his energies into passions that reveal his vibrant spirit and kind heart. His laughter, once a rare sound, now fills our home with warmth, a reflection of his journey from confusion and anger to a place of joy and self-assurance. His resilience has not only shaped his path but has also served as a reminder of the strength that lies in vulnerability and the courage required to embrace change.

As for Andrew and me, the transformation has been no less significant. Stepping into our roles as guardians has stretched the boundaries of our empathy, patience, and understanding, forging in us a deeper appreciation for the complexities of human emotions and the bonds that tie a family together. Our relationship, too, has been strengthened, tempered by the trials we've faced and enriched by the triumphs we've celebrated together.

The changes within our family structure have been profound. What began as an arrangement born of necessity has evolved into a deeply rooted bond, a connection that transcends the circumstances that brought us together. Our bonds have been strengthened not in spite of the challenges we've faced, but because of them. Through every hurdle and every moment of joy, we've woven a stronger, more resilient fabric of family, one that is built on the foundations of love, understanding, and shared growth.

This journey of growth and transformation has not only altered the course of our individual lives but has reshaped the essence of our family. It has taught us that family is not defined by blood alone but by the choices we make to support, to nurture, and to love one another, through the best and the worst of times. As we continue to evolve, these lessons in growth and transformation remain our guiding light, illuminating the path forward with hope and the promise of even deeper connections.

Navigating the unexpected journey that life thrust upon us, from the sudden expansion of our family to the myriad challenges that followed, has imparted lessons of invaluable depth and significance. Each obstacle, each moment of uncertainty, has been a teacher in its own right, offering insights that have profoundly shaped our understanding of resilience, empathy, and the transformative power of grace.

One of the most pivotal lessons learned is the true meaning of resilience. It's more than just the ability to withstand adversity; it's the courage to face the unknown with hope, to adapt and find strength not just within oneself but in the support and love of those around us. Resilience has been our beacon through the darkest nights, guiding us back to each other and forward into the light of new beginnings. It taught us that even when the path is uncharted, the journey can be navigated with determination and the belief that better days lie ahead.

Understanding, too, has been a cornerstone of our growth. The journey demanded that we listen not just with the intent to respond but to truly hear and empathize with each other's experiences and emotions. This deepened understanding has been the bridge over gaps of grief and misunderstanding, allowing us to connect in ways we never anticipated. It showed us that empathy is the key to unlocking the doors of communication and forging bonds that can withstand the tests of time and trial.

Above all, we learned the grace of giving and receiving forgiveness, of extending compassion not only to others but also to ourselves. Grace became our compass, guiding us through moments of frustration and misunderstanding, and reminding us of the beauty and strength found in forgiveness.

It taught us that healing is a journey of both letting go and holding on—letting go of pain and resentment, and holding on to love and the lessons each day brings.

These lessons—resilience, understanding, and grace—have become the pillars upon which our family stands. They have transformed our journey from one of unexpected challenges to a testament to the power of love and the enduring strength of the human spirit. As we continue to navigate the path that lies ahead, these insights remain our guiding lights, illuminating the way forward with hope and the promise of continued growth and deeper connections.

As we gaze toward the horizon, our family's collective vision for the future is painted with broad strokes of hope, ambition, and a steadfast commitment to continued growth, healing, and support. For each of us, this vision embodies not just personal aspirations but also our shared dreams, a testament to the journey we've undertaken together and the path we aspire to tread moving forward.

For Jack, our hope is that he continues to harness his resilience and sensitivity into avenues that foster his growth both personally and academically. We dream of a future for him filled with the fulfillment of his burgeoning interest in the arts, a space where his creativity can flourish unbounded by the shadows of the past. Our commitment to Jack is to provide the support he needs to explore these passions, encouraging him to embrace his unique journey of self-discovery and to cultivate the immense potential that lies within him.

John's path, bright and brimming with energy, holds the promise of exploration and discovery. Our vision for him is a life rich with opportunities to engage his boundless curiosity and spirit of adventure. We dream of a future where John's laughter continues to be a beacon of light in our home, a symbol of his journey from the depths of grief to the peaks of joy and fulfillment. Our pledge to John is to nurture this spark, to stand by him as he navigates the challenges of youth, and to celebrate each milestone he reaches on his path to becoming the compassionate, dynamic individual he is destined to be.

For Andrew and me, the future is envisioned as a continuation of our journey of partnership and mutual support, deepening the bonds that have been our anchor through the storms. Our dream is to cultivate a legacy of love and resilience, to be examples of strength and understanding for Jack and John, and to continue building a home that is a sanctuary of peace and growth. We are committed to our own paths of personal development, recognizing that our growth is inextricably linked to the well-being of our family.

Collectively, our vision for the future is one of unity, where each member's individual journey contributes to the strength and harmony of the whole. We dream of a future where our home continues to be a place of laughter, learning, and love, where the trials of the past are woven into the fabric of our resilience, and where our commitments to each other foster an environment of continuous support and healing.

Our hopes and dreams are buoyed by the knowledge that, together, we have navigated the unforeseeable with grace and strength. Looking forward, we step into the future with open hearts, ready to embrace the challenges and joys that await, secure in the love that binds us and the shared vision that guides us.

Conclusion:

As we draw the curtains on this chapter of our journey—a narrative woven with threads of resilience, hope, and an unwavering commitment to family unity—it's a moment to reflect on the essence of what we've shared and the universal truths that have emerged from our unique experience. Our story, marked by unforeseen challenges and unexpected roles, has been a testament to the strength of the human spirit and the boundless capacity for growth and adaptation.

Resilience has been the bedrock of our journey. It's a quality that was not inherent but forged in the crucible of adversity, a reminder that we are all capable of facing immense challenges and emerging stronger. This resilience was not just about enduring but about thriving—about finding joy and purpose in the midst of struggle and using our experiences to foster a deeper understanding of ourselves and the world around us.

Hope has been our guiding light, illuminating the path through our darkest days. It taught us that no matter how formidable the obstacles may seem, there is always a way forward. Hope inspired us to envision a future defined not by our past losses but by the possibilities that lie ahead. It's a force that propels us forward, encouraging us to dream, to aspire, and to create the life we wish to live.

Family unity, perhaps the most profound theme of our story, underscores the incredible strength found in togetherness. Our journey revealed that family is not just a bond of blood but a chosen commitment to love, support, and understand each other through every twist and turn of life. This unity, built on the foundation of shared experiences, challenges, and triumphs, has been our greatest source of strength and comfort.

To those who might be embarking on similar journeys, facing the uncertainties of life's unexpected turns, we offer these words of encouragement: Embrace the journey with all its imperfections, for it is in the challenges that we discover our true strength. Lean into the support of those around you, for it is in unity that we find our greatest resilience. Hold on to hope, for it is the beacon that guides us through the darkest nights.

Nest Refilled:
A Journey of Grit, Grace, and Renewal

Our experience, unique as it may be, reflects universal truths about the power of resilience, the gift of hope, and the strength of family unity. These truths, timeless and transcendent, remind us that even in the face of life's most daunting challenges, there is always a path forward, a possibility for growth, and a chance for renewal.

In closing, our story is a celebration of the human spirit, a tribute to the families who navigate the complexities of life with courage and love. It is a reminder that while our journeys may be fraught with challenges, they are also filled with moments of profound beauty and transformation. May our reflections serve as a source of hope and inspiration, encouraging all who read these words to embrace their journey with resilience, to foster unity in the face of adversity, and to hold fast to the hope that illuminates the path to a brighter future.

Nest Refilled:
A Journey of Grit, Grace, and Renewal

ABOUT THE AUTHOR

Omobonike Odegbami is a seasoned Higher Education Administrator with over two decades of experience, specializing in international education for the last 14 years. As a passionate advocate for social justice, she has dedicated her career to raising awareness of social justice issues both locally and globally. Through discussions and educational processes, she inspires personal responsibility and action to end oppression in all forms. Omobonike's work extends beyond traditional boundaries as she engages in innovative narratives that attempt to reframe public discourse around inclusion and belonging. Her commitment to fostering a sense of belonging and advocating for inclusive environments is evident in her contributions to higher education and her efforts to promote social justice. Omobonike has shared her journey of resilience and renewal in her book, "Nest Refilled; A Journey of Grit, Grace, and Renewal." She is a mother of two adul married and lives with her husband and 2 young boys in New Hartford, NY.

Printed in Great Britain
by Amazon